FOR THE MOON IS HOLLOW AND ALIENS RULE THE SKY

By

Rob Shelsky

For The Moon Is Hollow
And Aliens Rule The Sky

ISBN- 13: 978-1499172935
ISBN-10: 1499172931

PUBLISHED BY:
GKRS PUBLICATIONS
Copyright © 2014 by Rob Shelsky

All rights reserved. Without limiting the rights under copyright reserved above, no part of this publication may be reproduced, stored in or introduced into a retrieval system, or transmitted, in any form, or by any means (electronic, mechanical, photocopying, recording, or otherwise) without the prior written permission of both the copyright owners and the above publisher of this book.

This is a work of nonfiction. The author acknowledge the trademarked status and trademark owners of various products referenced in this work of nonfiction, which have been used without permission. The publication/use of these trademarks is not authorized, associated with, or sponsored by the trademark owners. All quotations and/or related materials are referenced either in the body of this book itself, or referenced at the end.

All works cited herein have their sources included. All illustrations/photos are courtesy Wikimedia Commons Public Domain images. Short portions of Public Domain documents, such as the Bible, etc., have been reproduced herein.

* * * * *

DEDICATED
IN MEMORIAM

TO

GEORGE A. KEMPLAND

Author, Friend, And So Very Much More

~1929 — 2013~

Wherever You Are Now, George,
May You Always Be Happy, At Peace,
And Enjoy Yourself Wherever You Are,
And I Hope I May Get To See You Again...
Somewhen.

Table of Contents

Section   **Page**

INTRODUCTION—A Hollow Moon And Aliens? 1
CHAPTER 1— Some Basic Facts About Our Moon.............7
CHAPTER 2—Possible Origins Of The Moon 11
CHAPTER 3—Problems With Current Idea
   Of Moon Formation 16
CHAPTER 4—Oddities Of The Moon 19
CHAPTER 5—Need More Moon Oddities? 25
CHAPTER 6—Idea Of A Hollow Moon 34
CHAPTER 7—Is The Moon Really Hollow? 39
CHAPTER 8—More Information About A Hollow Moon ...46
CHAPTER 9—Different Legs To Stand On.........................50
CHAPTER 10—Evidence Of Aliens From Astronauts.........60
CHAPTER 11—NASA COVERUP—"A Shadowy
   Government?" 71
CHAPTER 12—Ancient Evidence For A Time
   Before The Moon? 84
CHAPTER 13—Corroborating Evidence—Another
Hollow Moon?...91
CHAPTER 14—The Implications Of A Hollow Moon 101
CHAPTER 15—What's In A Hollow Moon?.......................105
CHAPTER 16—More On What's In A Hollow Moon.........114
CHAPTER 17—Was Mars A Failed Experiment? 120
CHAPTER 18—OUR Moon, An Alien Hollow World? 134
CHAPTER 19—Is There A "No Trespassing" Sign On The
   Moon? 138
CHAPTER 20—Who Warned Us Off The Moon? 146
CHAPTER 21—What Are Aliens Doing On The Moon?....155
CHAPTER 22—The Compelling Reason For
   Aliens To Come Here? 164
CHAPTER 23—Xenophobia And Hostility 171

Section	Page
CHAPTER 24—Maybe Xenophobic, But Still Alien Friends?	176
CHAPTER 25—How Long Have "They" Really Been Here?	183
CHAPTER 26—The Reason They're Here	194
CHAPTER 27—How Did The Moon Get Here?	203
CHAPTER 28—What To Make Of All This	206
ABOUT THE AUTHOR	213
REFERENCES	215

INTRODUCTION
A Hollow Moon And Aliens?

Many have written about the Moon in a variety of ways. Moreover, many speculations have been, and still are, made about our sister world, Earth's handmaiden of the night. Perhaps one of the strangest ideas mentioned is the idea of the Moon being hollow. Some have even promoted the notion the Moon is in reality an alien spaceship, an ancient one, and not a Moon as we think of one at all.

At the very least, they argue the Moon is hollow inside, as a spaceship would be. Of course, as night must follow day, the question then arises: if the Moon is just a shell, is it hiding something inside? And if so, just what is it concealing there?

Yes, this is a radical concept, of the Moon not only being hollow, but there being something strange, perhaps even something or someone of a terrifying nature hiding within the secrecy of its shell.

It must be said there are many who say this is even beyond a radical concept, and is, frankly, more in the realm of an absurd one. So is such an idea too incredible even to entertain? Is it just too bizarre even to be considered at all? As a researcher and UFO investigator, and one with an educational history firmly grounded in the hard sciences, including astronomy and geology, I originally found this idea very bizarre.

I have to admit, I felt the concept of a hollow Moon was even laughable. "Ludicrous," might be a better word. I put it right up there with those that still believed the Earth is flat. "Nut cases" are everywhere was my feeling, and so were conspiracy theorists. Find one and you'll find plenty of the other, as well.

Yet of all the Moons in our solar system, ours is definitely one of the more mysterious ones, if not the most mysterious of all. This much many of us already know. Although, some don't realize just how much this is really so and just how odd our Moon is.

Where we can explain the origins of practically every other moon in the solar system with comparative ease, we have far more trouble explaining our own satellite. Why is that, one wonders?

When we do come up with possible explanations for our Moon's origin, ones that seem reasonable at first glance, if a little lacking in some details at times perhaps, there always seem to be some complications with them later on. This keeps happening. This has happened with every single theory of the Moon's origin so far!

The question is, why? Why can't we come up with a simple theory, one that adequately explains the Moon being in our sky without having to resort to ever more elaborate additions to such theories to try to explain some rather glaring problems with them, some major inconsistencies? For some reason, we just can't.

Even our best current theory of the Moon's origin can't account for some of the quirkier things we know about the Moon. This, in itself, is highly curious and not just a little suspicious, because as mentioned above, the origins of moons of other planets in our solar system don't seem to be nearly so problematic, or so decidedly bizarre in nature.

Why is it the one world in our solar system that supports life and intelligent life (as we consider ourselves to be, although some may have good reason to dispute this idea), Earth, also has such a mysterious and oversized Moon? Is this just mere coincidence? Or might there be more to all of this than we realize, then we should just take for granted?

What is more, for a supposedly dead world, an airless chunk of rock that "just happens" to orbit our planet, strange things seem to happen there and often. NASA itself commissioned a report that spans centuries and that contains numerous transient lunar phenomena (meaning unexplained strange events), as they call them. These have occurred on the Moon during that time, and long before, as it turns out.

This document, an officially commissioned one for NASA is dealt with in depth in our prior book, ***DARKER SIDE OF THE MOON "They Are watching Us!*** However, if you prefer the basic document without the analysis we provided along with it, you could find it online at: http://www.astrosurf.com/luxorion/ltp-r277-index.htm.

Even a quick review of this document, one including the last five hundred years of observations of weird events on the Moon (again, referred to by the compilers of the report as "transient lunar phenomena"), will tell anyone that very bizarre things, indeed, have been going on for a long time on our Moon.

For a dead world then, it doesn't seem to be very dead at all. In fact, it appears to be just the opposite, a highly active place at times, and an extremely mysterious one, as well.

Then there are the conspiracy theories concerning NASA hiding evidence of aliens being on the Moon, and of such beings having been there in ages past. Some of this evidence is rather telling. It has been put forth by reliable people, persons either who worked directly for NASA, or who indirectly were in positions of trust as contractors to NASA.

These are not people lightly dismissed as just "fringe" elements, or "dyed-in-the-wool" conspiracy theorists. They have bona fide credentials. They have good work histories and solid reputations in every other respect.

To claim such things not only jeopardized their jobs, but hurt their reputations, as well. Few people would do this for a short-term notoriety and just a small monetary gain. Weighing that against a long-term, well-paying career just wouldn't make sense. So why did they make these claims? Well, the answer is because they truly believe them.

These people speak of airbrushed photographs given to the public. They talk of other pictures NASA has completely denied the public access to in any way. These people claim such pictures show evidence of alien bases on the Moon, past and present, and of a current alien presence there. Some even claim we have been "warned off the Moon." Several noted Ufologists believe this, as well, as odd as the idea might sound.

Besides this, there are those tantalizing and intriguing pieces of evidence with regard to aliens not only being in space near Earth, but on the Moon, as well. Our own astronauts have provided this evidence. Although often inadvertently, but sometimes on purpose, it seems, the public has become aware of outlandish events happening in space. We even have actual recordings of astronauts referring to "alien spaceships."

Then, of course, there are the constant sightings of UFOs in our own skies here on Earth. Millions around the world have claimed to see them.

Fact: Over one million reports of UFO sightings flood in annually on a worldwide basis.

Fact: UFOs have appeared in our heavens throughout our history, as well.

Fact: Over two million persons claim to have been abducted by such craft in recent decades alone.

Fact: People have been hurt in UFO encounters, sickened, and some even killed!

So the question naturally arises, just what does this all mean? Could the Moon actually be hollow? Could it be an ancient alien spacecraft disguised as just a moon?

Are we being watched "closely" and "keenly" by alien intelligences? Are they using the Moon as a massive base of operations in our solar system? Have we been warned away from approaching the Moon too closely, as far as actual manned landings there go?

We should note here that even the most recent unmanned robotic landing, in December 2013, the "Jade Rabbit," and one made by the Chinese, has quickly ceased to function correctly. It has so far failed to even come close to completing its planned mission as a result. The reason for this is unknown, although various guesses have been made. The Jade Rabbit, it seems, suffers from "mechanical issues." This is a vague and unsatisfying explanation at best.

So some very strange things exist about our Moon and with regard to our Moon. In this book, we want to concentrate on the Moon itself, and try to find out what exactly is going on there. Is the Moon hollow? Is it an alien spaceship? Are there alien bases on the Moon? If not now, were there once such bases, perhaps long ago? What is their purpose in being there? What do they, or did they once want?

As you can see, there are many questions. And there are equally many explanations and theories to account for them, to try to find answers. Along with more mundane explanations conspiracy theories flourish, as well.

However, is there any evidence to support such seemingly eccentric contentions? If so, just what does that mean for us if there is any truth to them? What are the implications for our future, if aliens were once on the Moon and/or may still be there even now? How does it affect us right now? What are the consequences for our plans for future space exploration if any of this might be true? For instance, can we have a Moon base, or is that "forbidden" to us?

As you can see, not only do we have questions about the Moon and a multitude of theories to try to answer them, but even the answers seem to raise more questions for us. So sorting through all this is no easy task. Of course, one could reduce all those questions to one main one: just what is going on with the Moon?

In this book, For the Moon Is Hollow and Aliens Rule the Sky we intend to try to find out, to take a much deeper look at the Moon with regard to all this and the idea aliens may somehow be involved. We intend to focus on the question as to whether the Moon is an alien base, perhaps even hollow, and maybe even being an alien spaceship. We want to know if there is real evidence for aliens inhabiting our sister world, or having once inhabited it in the past. We want to try to find some answers to all these questions regarding the Moon.

Finally, if the Moon is an alien base, are there other such bases in our solar system? And if so, who really rules our solar system, controls the skies? Is it "them or us?" The answer to this question just might surprise you.

We have to warn you, prying into our mysterious Moon might just give you answers you'd rather not hear, ones you might not wish to think about, so proceed with caution. And if you think the idea of a hollow Moon is a fantasy, wait until you read some of the evidence we've discovered.

Yes, we thought the idea of a hollow Moon was something to laugh at, only something cranks and conspiracy theorists could possibly believe was true. Now, we're not nearly so sure. In the next chapters, we will explain why.

Let us proceed to look at this all in more detail, see if we can't just figure out what might be going on with "our" Mysterious Moon.

CHAPTER 1

Some Basic Facts About Our Moon

Just why is our Moon such a mysterious world? Why is it that of all the moons in our solar system, the one just a mere quarter of a million miles away from us, the one that rules our night sky and can be seen so clearly by us, is probably the most bizarre of all the moons in the solar system? What is it about our airless and so-called dead Moon that is so strange?

Well, to begin with, let's consider what we know about the Moon right now, the basic "facts," as scientists like to call them.

Fact 1: The first thing to know about the Moon, the one causing the most problems for the average person, that trips them up the most, is one face of the Moon is always towards the Earth.

This means from Earth we can't see the other side of the Moon. This other side has been commonly known as the "dark side of the Moon." This is a common fallacy and just wrong. Probably, this idea of a dark side of the moon is due at least in part to the music band, Pink Floyd, and their Dark Side of the Moon album, which was such a hit at one time.

Still, in reality this term is a misnomer, because it is not the dark side, a side of the Moon permanently wrapped in night, as it were. All sides of the Moon get sunlight, just as the Earth does. The Moon does have a day and night, with the daytime, as well as the nighttime, each being about fourteen of our days in length.

One full day on the Moon is about twenty-eight days here on Earth. Roughly this is the equivalent of one month (one "moonth" as it was once known).

During that time, as daylight moves slowly across the surface of the Moon, we see it as phases of the Moon in the night sky, as more or less area of the surface of our neighbor is lit by sunlight, with the Moon waxing (becoming full), and waning (reducing to a new Moon).

Therefore, the term, "far side," of the Moon is much more appropriate rather than "dark side." There is a reason why we stress the far side of the Moon here, and it's another one of those "mysteries" we wish to discuss later on, one concerning the thickness of the crust there.

However, because we only see one face of the Moon, the one always facing our Earth, this meant that for most of the time we've been on this planet, humans simply didn't know what the far side of the Moon looked like. It was never revealed to us. Therefore, in a sense it was "dark," but dark as in us having no knowledge of it.

Thanks to photographs from various NASA missions to our nearest neighbor, and those from satellites launched by other nations, in the last decades we think we have developed a good idea of what the far side of the Moon does look like. I say "think," because there is a big question about those photographs.

One thing scientists immediately noticed about the far side is there seem to be a lot more craters there than on the side facing us. Just another one of those "mysteries," it seems. Again, we will discuss this subject in more detail later on. Nevertheless, already you can see there are some odd things about the Moon we just don't understand.

A few more facts:

Fact 2. The average distance to the Moon from the Earth is roughly 238,900 miles. In kilometers this equals just about 384,000.

Fact 3. So close is the Moon to us, it is thought of by many as not so much as being just a satellite of Earth, but rather as one part of a double-planet system. In other words, to a certain degree, the Moon doesn't just revolve around us, but we orbit more like a spinning dumbbell around each other.

Fact 4. If one considers all the moons of the solar system, then our Moon ranks as the fifth largest. The mass of the Moon is about 1/80th of the Earth's. By mass, we're talking about the material that composes our nearest neighbor, its density. This means gravity on the Moon is only one sixth, approximately, of Earth.

It's important here that we don't confuse the idea of "mass" with that of "weight." Weight is something defined by a gravity field. For instance, you have a certain amount of mass and if you step on the scales on Earth, you will "weigh" a certain amount. However, on the Moon, although you will have exactly the same mass, you will only weigh one sixth as much. Mass stays the same, therefore, but weight does not. We stress this here, because later on we will be referring to this with regard to the Hollow Moon Theory.

Yet, just a few more facts about the Moon and then we'll move on:

Fact 5. The diameter of the Moon, that is the span of it from one edge to the other, is roughly equivalent to the width of the United States, just a little less.

Fact 6. The Moon orbits the Earth at a speed of about 2,300 miles per hour. This is the equivalent of 3,700 km.

Fact 7. The surface of the Moon has numerous craters pockmarking it. Some of these craters are quite large, being huge. And there are craters within craters, newer ones on top of the older existing ones. This helps us to determine the age of craters. Older ones tend to have newer ones on top of them.

Fact 8. There are also areas called *maria* (from the Latin, meaning, "seas"). They are not seas, of course. The Moon is airless, has almost no air, and only traces of water. Rather, they are large, relatively flat areas, darkly colored ones. These are thought to be old lava flows. The Moon also has mountains, with crater walls often resembling such mountains in height.

Fact 9. Temperatures on the Moon can range from being 243° F. in the daytime, to a -272° F. at night. This is a huge range in temperature, a drastic one.

Fact 10. That the Moon's mass exerts a pull of the Earth is known by just about everybody. This pull results in tides, of course. And this, too, figures later on in our discussion about the possibility of the Moon being hollow, because if it isn't, then how to account for the calculated mass of the moon?

CHAPTER 2

Possible Origins Of The Moon

Now we come to the age and supposed origin of the Moon. We say, "supposed," because these are really theories only, rather than facts, and in actuality, there are five main theories. Again, the reason for this is we simply don't know which one of them is correct. They are:

1. The Theory of Capture. Up until the time of the 1980s, this theory was probably the most widely accepted idea of how the Moon came to be with the Earth. The premise is simple. The Moon was a wandering planetary body that was later captured by the Earth, locked into orbit around our planet.

This theory has some advantages. It explains the large size of the Moon. It had nothing to do with Earth, but just wandered by and was captured. This theory also has the advantage of explaining the Moon's orbit and the fact only one face of the Moon is turned always towards the Earth, because it is tidally locked in position that way. In other words, Earth just grabbed the Moon as a companion and kept it.

Problems with the Capture Theory. There are problems with this idea. For one thing, any satellite, such as the Moon, or any planet wandering so close to the Earth is more likely to collide with the planet, or cause resulting wild orbits for both, and one or the other of the two worlds getting sent off on a tangent, maybe even sailing out of our solar system for good.

Furthermore, this whole theory rests on the idea the early Earth must've had a very extensive atmosphere at one time. It had to have reached much further out to space than it does now. This could have acted as friction, a brake on the Moon. It then slowed it enough so that it could be "captured" and allowed to go into orbit around our world, instead of ending up in one of those other two possibilities—collision, or sent off into space, never to be seen again. Another problem with this theory is we have absolutely no evidence the Earth's atmosphere ever extended so far into space. We just see no supporting or corroborative evidence for this idea at all.

More Problems with Theory of Capture. One of them is the oxygen-ratio of rocks found on the Moon. They are almost identical to that of Earth's, and this would seem unlikely, if the Moon had come from somewhere else.

Each planet and planetoid, even asteroids, all have unique oxygen-ratio "signatures" to their rocks, their physical makeup. These can be very accurately measured. So the fact of the Moon being captured and having the exact same signature as minerals on Earth, just seems very improbable. Almost all scientists now discount this idea of a "captured Moon" and think it is just wrong.

There is also the whole idea of the Capture Theory just being an incredible one, one hard to believe. No less a famous person, scientist and author, than Isaac Asimov, stated:

"It's [the Moon] too big to have been captured by the Earth. The chances of such a capture having been effected and the Moon then having taken up nearly circular orbit around our Earth are too small to make such an eventuality credible."

Therefore, the Capture Theory has major problems and ones which some very famous, learned, and respected people have severe doubts about being possible at all. In short, nobody really buys the theory as credible anymore.

2. The Theory of Accretion. This theory accounts for the oxygen-ratio problem by saying that both worlds formed out of the early accretion disk, those rings of rubble that slowly formed planets during the early stages of the creation of our solar system. The Earth and Moon became a double-planet system, one born of the same material.

Problems with Theory of Accretion. Yes, again we have problems with this theory, as well and major ones. If the Moon and Earth formed as a double planet system to begin with, this does not explain the problem of the angular momentum.

Don't let that term throw you. It simply means the degree of rotation any given body has. The Earth rotates on its axis and this is angular momentum. What's more, the Accretion Theory doesn't explain why the Moon has such a small iron core, comparatively speaking, to that of the Earth. They should be more proportional if the theory is valid, but they simply are not. So this theory doesn't work too well either. In fact, most scientists don't think it's correct.

3. The Theory of Fission. This is a very old theory and dates back to Charles Darwin. This theory states the early Earth was spinning so quickly, that due to centrifugal force, it literally threw off a piece of itself, which later became the Moon. The Pacific basin was considered the place where this might have happened and that it was literally a "hole" left by the Moon leaving the early Earth.

Problems with Theory of Fission. Although the theory accounts for why the Moon has the same oxygen-isotope ratio as rocks on Earth do, we now know the Pacific basin is the result of continental drift, and not because the Moon blasted away from it.

Also, there is the problem of age. The material that makes up the Moon is far older than the crust in the region of the Pacific basin, or anywhere else, for that matter. Furthermore, the theory does not explain away the angular momentum problem, either. So again, we have a largely discredited theory.

4. The theory of a Georeactor Explosion. This is an interesting theory. It hypothesizes the Moon is the result of a "georeactor" exploding deep in the Earth, where the mantle meets the core.

Again, don't let the term "Georeactor" throw you. Nuclear reactors are possible because of radioactive elements. Put enough radioactive material too close together and you get "critical mass." This just means you have enough material, in close enough proximity to other such similar material, to cause a chain reaction resulting in an explosion, or if controlled in the production of energy, as with nuclear reactors producing electricity. Of course, as we've found out with the Chernobyl and Fukushima meltdowns, sometimes even these get out of control.

A georeactor is just a naturally occurring one of these, where by chance there is enough fissionable material in close enough proximity to trigger such a "natural" explosion.

For this to work in order to create the Moon, it had to have happened right at the equatorial plane of the Earth. In other words, it had to be close to the region of the equator.

Moreover, it must have been a big explosion, a very big one. Obviously, there would seem to be some problems with this theory, with such a coincidence being just one of them, but it does explain some things, as well. It explains why the Moon is made up of the same material as the mantle layer of the Earth, for instance.

Problems with Georeactor Theory. However, the theory does present other problems. For instance, there is the problem with angular momentum, the orbit of the moon, etc. They aren't the predicted results for such an event. This theory is a very new one, by the way, only first proposed in 2010.

5. The Theory of a Giant Impact. According to many scientists, the most reliable theory of the Moon's origin is that a planet or protoplanet (referred to as "Theia") just about the size of Mars, struck the Earth early on, about 4.36 billion years ago, during the still formative period of the solar system and the Earth.

The impact was catastrophic, almost resulted in destroying the Earth in the process, and threw material out into a ring around our young world. This material quickly, and we mean very quickly, supposedly coalesced into the Moon. Again, this is known as the "Giant Impact Theory."

Mind you, this is only a theory, the best scientists can come up with for now, because it explains some of the things about the Moon. But just as with the other theories, not all things can be explained, unfortunately. We will discuss this more later. In any case, our Moon formed out of this ring of material, coalesced into a molten ball in what many scientists say had to be in just a hundred years or less in time.

Problems with Giant Impact Theory. There are a number of them and they are large ones, as well. We will discuss them in more depth later on, but just as an example, if this happened, surely there should have been some material from the original Theia composing the Moon, as well as material from Earth? There doesn't seem to be any material from Theia, in fact.

If the scenario is valid, if two worlds collided, smashed apart, and then reformed, this just doesn't seem to be a likely result. The Moon should have, some say must have, material from Theia in order for this theory to be true. There are other ramifications, as well, and we will discuss them a little later on.

Chapter Conclusion. Why is all this important to us here? Well, again, there are some problems with all these theories, some major ones, and they affect our coming discussion of what the Moon is or really may be.

Now, we'll look in closer detail at just what the problems are with the current theory, and why it may not be valid at all. Then we'll discuss just what may be a good, if controversial alternative, and that is the Hollow Moon Theory.

CHAPTER 3

Problems With Current Idea Of Moon Formation

As the title of this chapter suggests, there are problems with our current most popular theory, the Giant Impact Theory, about how the Moon formed. These problems are major ones. Again, they are important to us here, because they tell us there may be another origin for the Moon, an entirely different one.

As we mentioned earlier, the current and widely popular theory is the Moon is the result of a Mars-sized planet impacting the early Earth. This produced a ring of debris, which quickly clumped together into a molten ball that became our Moon. This sounds eminently reasonable, but as with all such things concerning the Moon, if this is how it truly formed, then one should expect certain outcomes as a result. For instance, if this was so, then:

1. As mentioned at the end of the last chapter, the Moon's makeup of material should include some of the impacting planet's (Theia's) material, as well as that of Earth's. However, rocks brought back from the Moon show this just does not seem to be the case. The Apollo missions brought hundreds of pounds of rocks from various locations back, and the oxygen isotopic ratio of those rocks seems to be identical to Earth's.

The likelihood that the impacting planet, Theia, had exactly the same isotopic ratio as Earth does is vanishingly small. So if the

Moon is made up of debris from Theia and Earth, it should have material from both worlds there, with distinctly different oxygen isotopic ratios.

Very oddly, it does not. Even harder to understand is the Moon's Titanium ratio turns out to be almost the same as Earth's, as well (it is within four parts per million), and this, too, seems to show the Moon is not made up of any of Theia's material at all.

How can this be? When two such planetary bodies collide, literally trillions of tons of material should have been ejected into space as either molten and/or vaporized material from both worlds. They should have intermingled. In short, the space around the Earth should have been a mess of debris from both worlds, impossible to separate out.

Yet our Moon seems to only possess material from Earth. Why is that so if the theory is correct? It's a major problem, obviously, a very major one, indeed.

2. There is the question of the volatile elements still left on the Moon. Again, don't let that term, "volatile elements," bother you. It simply means substances that are very likely to vaporize under high temperature conditions, and boil away into space, such as water.

Now the material making up the Moon is low in such volatile ingredients. This would be expected if the Moon was a ball of molten magma in the early stages of its formation. In fact, it would be surprising if this was not the actual case under such formative conditions.

However, the volatile elements on the Moon are still higher than one would expect for this. The amount of water in rocks on the Moon is too high, and should have had far more boiled away in the early stages of the Moon's development.

3. The crust of the lunar surface on the far side is thicker than the crust on the side closest to Earth. Scientists have attempted to explain this by saying there was a secondary and later impact on the Moon by another moonlet left over and in the same orbit.

Of course, this begins to make the theory a rather complex one, somewhat unwieldy, and all the shakier every time you have to "fix" it more. It's almost as if, as the theory begins to fail them, the scientists keep adding bits and pieces to it, in order to shore it up.

What they often end up with, metaphorically speaking, is an unwieldy house of cards that threatens to collapse on them at any moment. In this case, it's a planet colliding, the Moon coalescing from the debris (without any of Theia's remnants in it at all), and then another moonlet striking the new Moon on the far side. Hmm… definitely getting hard to accept at this point.

Chapter Conclusion. So as we can plainly see, although all these theories have their advantages, they have distinct disadvantages, as well, even the currently most popular and accepted one. They have problems, some of them truly big ones.

Although scientists are willing to go to great lengths to prop up their favorite theories, even then there are still problems with them. What does this result in? Well, scientists the world over keep coming up with new theories as a result, attempts to better explain the origin of our Moon, as with the Georeactor Theory, which again, was only formulated in 2010-2012. Yet, no one theory is satisfactory. This is the reason they come and go in favor with scientists over the decades, rather like going in and out of fashion.

However, they do show our Moon is very odd compared to most others in the solar system, and even elsewhere, in other stellar systems, because we simply can't readily account for its creation. No matter how it formed, whatever theory above may be correct, if any of them are, it certainly is a strange way for our Moon to have originated.

There are other strange things about the Moon, other oddities, as well, and we will discuss those in the next chapter.

CHAPTER 4

Oddities Of The Moon

Besides the distinctly odd origins of the Moon, whatever they may actually be, there are other strange things about the Moon, things that are very bizarre.

An oddity. For one thing, the latest dating of the Moon rocks would seem to indicate the Moon is younger than we thought. Dating samples, more accurate ones, show the Moon is only 4.36 billion years old. This is much younger than the original estimates of 4.44 to 4.567 billion years in age.

What does this mean? Well, either the Moon formed much later on, or there was no sea of molten magma involved in its formation. This last seems unlikely. The lunar rocks are so depleted of hydrates; this shows they underwent a great heat and so must have melted to liquid magma.

Estimates are that during the collision of the two planets, Theia crashing into the Earth, temperatures could have been as high as 18,000° in some areas of the explosion. This would vaporize any volatile constituents of the rocks. Certainly, the surface of the Moon should have been all magma, hot liquid rock at one point, as a consequence of such a catastrophic collision. Yet, the theory requires Theia to have impacted Earth much earlier on.

Oddity of no volcanoes. The *maria* on the Moon, those large dark "seas" of lunar material are supposed to be from magma, molten rock. Yet, there seem to be no volcanoes on the Moon. There should be at least long-extinct ones if the Moon ever had a molten core.

How could there have been these vast fields of lava (magma) upwelling from a molten interior, but not a single volcano anywhere on the Moon as a side effect of such vast geologic activity, as well? And to date, no volcanoes have been discovered on the Moon. This is a major oddity, and a very strange one.

Also, how do we account for the Moon's relatively young age compared to that of the Earth? Right now, scientists simply can't account for this. Oh, there are a plethora of theories, but none of them really seems to make any sense yet. Something is definitely wrong with the theory if this is so.

Another oddity. This isn't a small one, either. There is the oddity of the orbit of the Moon around the Earth. It is almost perfectly circular. Why is this strange? Well, almost all orbits of planets are elliptical, being sort of a slightly squashed circle in shape.

Even planets found orbiting other star systems, and we have found at least a couple thousand of those already so far, have elliptical orbits. So, in other words, the Moon is not only in a strange orbit by our solar system's standards, but it's even strange for any other solar system, as well, apparently.

Why is this so? Again, there are many theories, but none seem to adequately explain it well. There are flaws, big ones, inherent in all of them.

Another oddity about the Moon's circular orbit. Because of the nature of the orbit, the Moon's center of gravity does not align with its geometric center. It is off by some 6,000 feet, well over a mile (1,828.8 meters, approximately).

What does this mean? Well, by all rights, the Moon should have a pronounced wobble as a result of this fact. Yet, amazingly, it doesn't. And this causes a slight bulge, and where is that bulge? Well, it is on the far side of the Moon.

The oddity of the Moon's convenient diameter and the solar eclipse. Peculiarly, and highly coincidentally, the Moon's diameter, combined with its distance from Earth allows our sister world to perfectly blot out the sun during a solar eclipse. This is just another one of those "oddities," it seems, because no other planet in our solar system has a moon that will do this anywhere nearly so perfectly. Even Isaac Asimov made the comment:

"There is no astronomical reason why the moon and the sun should fit so well. It is the sheerest of coincidences, and only the Earth among all the planets is blessed in this fashion."

Blessed, indeed; an odd choice of words for Isaac Asimov to have used. It implies this is just short of being a miracle. And on the one planet in the system with intelligent life that can use such a "blessing" to such great advantage to learn things about our universe around us. Just another coincidence?

Yet another oddity. Mind you, in order to have such a nearly perfect orbit, the Moon had to have a very particular velocity and approach angle to start with, as it came to us. The chances of that happening, are again, very small, almost vanishingly so. This is just one more oddity, for it seems no matter how strange, how small a chance of all these things occurring, somehow they did come about, they "somehow" all just happened. Coincidences seem to be compounding themselves here.

The truly bizarre oddity of the bell effect. There is something else very weird about the Moon. It was first recognized with the lunar Landers, and once having done their job, having been allowed to crash back onto the surface of the Moon. The result of these crashes was a phenomenon known as "resonance."

In simpler words and wholly unexpectedly, the Moon rang like the proverbial "bell." (And bells are hollow.) Actually, some resonance is to be expected. Even when solid rock is struck, it tends to vibrate, but not like this!

This "resonance" or ringing went on for a very long time. On November 20, 1969, which was the first time, the Moon "rang" for over an hour! Subsequently, when a portion of the Apollo 13 rocket, the third stage, struck the lunar surface, the Moon rang again, this time for over three hours! A ringing bell, indeed.

The vibrations went as deep as 25 miles. Lunar seismographs, left on the Moon to record seismographic events, such as possible moonquakes, recorded this. This vibrating implies there could well be no lunar core at all.

One more oddity. According to scientists, the Moon has no magnetic field surrounding it, unlike the Earth, which does. Our magnetic field is powerful and helps protect our planet from the solar wind, all those charged particles that would otherwise strike the Earth and cause damage to our biosphere and ultimately act to blow away our atmosphere.

This lack of a magnetic field surrounding the Moon also makes many scientists think the Moon has no core, or if it does, that it is solid and not molten, as the Earth's is.

What's more, if the Moon is like Mars (and many scientists think this is so) in this regard, then neither world has a molten core, since Mars, too, lacks a magnetosphere. The current theory is that such a molten core is required to create magnetic fields around a planet.

Furthermore, scientists think this is the reason Mars has long since lost much of its atmosphere, due to the unobstructed pressure of the solar wind (again, not really a "wind" as we know it, but instead a field of moving charged particles), literally blowing it away over time, because there was no magnetosphere to protect it, as here on Earth.

However, some scientists have found an interaction with the solar wind and certain areas on the Moon. They describe these areas as possibly being "mini magnetospheres" on the surface of the Moon, because of this effect.

One research study said there seems to be evidence for the existence of one such magnetosphere, for example, in the Reiner Gamma area on the Moon. What would cause such mini magnetospheres is unknown. Scientists cannot readily account for them.

One suggestion is they are the result of large meteor impacts, which somehow created magnetic anomalies on the Moon. However, the magnetospheres don't seem to be at these crater sites, but on the opposite side of the Moon from them.

It's hard to imagine such an effect being felt some 2,000 miles away from a meteor impact, and on the opposite side of the Moon from those impacts. If magnetospheres are a result of such strikes, they should be much more localized to those regions where the impacts occurred. So just what does account for them? Scientists simply have no real idea.

Oddity of Magnetic rocks on Moon. An oddity about the rocks brought back from the Moon is they were magnetized. Why is this an oddity? Well, as mentioned above, the Moon has no magnetic field, so without one, the rocks shouldn't all be magnetized. Maybe some, those found locally in the area of those "mini magnetospheres," but certainly not all. Scientists simply aren't able to account for the lunar material being so magnetized. This is just one more bizarre problem in a long list of them now.

Helium 3 Oddity on the Moon. Unlike on Earth, there is, apparently, a great deal of Helium 3 on the Moon. Helium 3 is simply helium molecules made up of three atoms of Helium, but again, this is a rarity on the Earth.

Estimates indicate there may be as much or even more than 1,100,000 tons of Helium 3 on the Moon. This is a phenomenal amount, but it has incredible implications. You see, Helium 3 is the ideal fuel for fusion power, which is even now in its later stages of development, with some real success in that endeavor being achieved in just the last few years.

As a fuel, about 100 tons of Helium 3 would supply all of us on Earth with enough energy for an entire year. So if we do develop successful fusion power plants, the demand for Helium 3 will be great. And the Moon would be the best available source of such fuel and in great quantities.

But maybe, we aren't the first to discover the Moon as being a great source of this fuel? Some claim, and even show photographs to back such statements, that there were once (and could still be) alien mining operations on the surface of the Moon. Were they mining for Helium 3?

CHAPTER 5

Need More Moon Oddities?

As if all these weird things about the moon aren't enough, there are—you guessed it—even more. Here are just some of them:

The oddity of moonquakes. This is a particularly strange oddity, even strange by the Moon's standards for such things. During the Apollo missions from 1969 to 1972, and as mentioned earlier, seismic recorders were installed, left behind on the Moon. No one at the time thought this meant very much, that there would be any actual results.

However, contrary to this idea, there were results, and lots of them. There have been literally hundreds of moonquakes, some reaching as high as 5.5 on the Richter Scale. Considering the Moon has no tectonic plates, no continental drift, and probably a frozen core, scientists couldn't understand how this could be. Moonquakes must be caused by something other than what causes them on Earth. Just what that "something" is, scientists can only conjecture.

The current and most prevalent theory for the cause of moonquakes is tidal forces exerted on the Moon by the pull of the Earth. However, there are some major problems with this theory. (When it comes to the Moon, it seems there always are.)

The biggest problem being that although the tidal pulls are always the same on a month-to-month basis, the quakes only seem to occur in other regions, those NOT predicted to be affected by the tides. Scientists can't account for why this is so.

The reason for deep moonquakes is also a mystery. In short, the whole moonquake problem is a mystery, an enigma scientists are still attempting to solve. In other words, as to just what causes these quakes, is still, ultimately, unknown.

In fact, as one scientist put it, the whole question of the interior of the Moon is pretty "sketchy." Not exactly a scientific explanation, but an honest one, it seems.

One thing that is known is there was a "nest" of thirty deep moonquakes on the far side of the Moon. However, according to the scientists, these "deep" quakes don't seem to go as far down as the core, or somehow were deflected around the core.

As one research paper states: *"...the deep interior of the Moon severely attenuates or deflects seismic waves."* How solid rock or an iron core could accomplish this is utterly unknown to scientists, for the normal type of core, too, should transmit the quake shockwaves, as well.

However, if there were no core at all, and the center was hollow, there would be nothing there to transmit such shockwaves and they would have to go "around" the hollow space, instead. So is there a core, or is it hollow? Based on moonquakes, scientists just don't know, but a hollow interior would account for the quakes' deflection around the center of the Moon.

Oddity of the Moon's crust being harder than thought. This oddity was almost funny; because it resulted in the first astronauts to land on the Moon having a heck of time getting lunar rock samples, so hard was the crust. When trying to drill, the astronauts were literally in danger of lofting themselves off the surface in the light gravity, so strenuous were their efforts to obtain samples, to be able to drill into the resistant rock of one of the *maria* on the Moon.

Just why the lunar surface rock is so much harder than scientists had expected, or taken into consideration in designing methods of retrieving rocks samples, is just one more bizarre oddity.

Oddity of Crust of Moon being thicker on the Far Side than on the near side. As mentioned earlier, the far side of the Moon has a thicker crust than the nearer side. This is very peculiar, for the Earth does not have this sort of anomaly, nor any other moon or planet we know of in our solar system. The planetary impact theory of Theia with Earth goes to elaborate extra lengths to account for this by adding another Moon or moonlet in orbit around the Earth, which subsequently collided with the main one. Again, this makes for an unwieldy theory and presents other problems as to how this could have happened.

Weird oddity of strange elements that shouldn't be there. As it also turns out, the samples of lunar rocks were largely made up of ilmenite, a dark, metal oxide mineral, and one rich in Titanium. Titanium is a popular metal because of its lightness, strength, durability, and hardness. It is also an expensive metal, because of its relative rarity and cost of refining.

Apparently, the Moon, "oddly" enough, has plenty of it, although on Earth, it isn't nearly so plentiful. Also, lunar samples contained Neptunium 237, as well as Uranium 236, elements not found on Earth to any real extent.

Neptunium 237 is found only in trace quantities here on Earth as a result of radioactive decay of Uranium, but it is unstable, and because it decays, this is why there is so little of it on Earth. Uranium 236, although more stable than Uranium 238 (hot radioactive), is rare on Earth for the same reason. It, too, decays.

So why is there so much of it on the Moon? This is a mystery, because the only way we can obtain it in any quantity is through artificial, "manmade" means here on our world. In other words, here on Earth, if we want it, we have to make it. Is it natural on the Moon for some reason, but not here, or did somebody have to "make" it there, as well?

Apparent oddity of a swirling pattern of craters at the Lunar South Pole. There is an odd sort of visual in a photograph taken through the auspices of NASA and it's a strange sort of picture. Please go to:

http://www.solarviews.com/cap/Moon/clmsouth.htm. The photograph is of the South Lunar Pole and it appears to show a definite swirling pattern, a spiral, if you will, that centers on the South Pole. From there, the craters seem to "swirl" outward in a counterclockwise direction, a spiral pattern.

The question is if this is just an optical illusion, or something real. To us, it certainly looks real enough, but you can judge for yourselves by looking at the photo. The photo, by the way, is a compilation of smaller, regional photos, assembled into the larger one, but no trickery or "retouching" was involved in that assembly. NASA assembles such photos all the time.

Fog bank or cloud oddity on Moon. Strangely, monitoring instruments left behind on the Moon to collect data registered a "cloud" of water vapor. This occurred March 7, 1971. This "cloud" drifted over the lunar surface, and remained detectable for 14 hours, approximately. The "cloud" encompassed approximately 100 square miles. On the Moon, there is supposed to be virtually no atmosphere at all, being a near vacuum there, so finding water vapor in such an amount is very odd.

Ancient and modern oddities cited in NASA Technical Report R-277 "Chronological Catalog of Reported Lunar Events." We published a copy of this entire and lengthy report in our sister book, *DARKER SIDE OF THE MOON "They" Are Watching Us!* Briefly and as mentioned, the report, compiled at the behest of NASA, dates back to 1500 B.C.E and up to relatively recent times, the mid-1960s, and covers some five hundred years of lunar oddities.

This period was chosen because it starts with when the telescope first began to be used and such use became ever more prevalent with each succeeding century. Apparently, the premise was that with the help of telescopes, such observations would be more reliable.

However, the reports of strange events on the Moon date back far earlier than just this period. Even so, the observers include many truly famous names in science and astronomy, their credentials, therefore, being impeccable.

Just what did they see on the Moon? Well, we can't go into it as in-depth as we did with the other book, but you name it, it seems someone saw it. Everything from "lightning," "glows," "streaks," "mists," "vapors," "beacons," "pulses of light," "moving lights," "volcanoes," "beams," "clouds," "tracks," and more, have been observed. These have been seen not only repeatedly, but sometimes for long durations, extending for months, and so witnessed by far more than just one lone astronomer of the times.

So common are these sightings, even now, NASA has coined the term "Transient Lunar Phenomena" to describe them. However, this is a catchall phrase, and includes every kind of sighting mentioned above.

But what are they? Naming something doesn't really tell us what it is. As just one example, take "volcano" sightings on the moon. Of course, scientists have determined if there were ever volcanoes on the Moon, they ceased well over a billion or more years ago. So just what the "volcanoes" seen on the Moon in the report are, remains a total mystery. Yet many astronomers according to the report, observed them, or at least called something they saw by that name.

Oddity of Moon blinks. NASA's own "Operation Moon Blink" shocked officials when it actually managed to spot no less than 28 strange events on the Moon in a very brief span of time.

"Rosetta Stone of the planets" oddity. This is a reference by Dr. Robert Jastrow. He was a chairman (the first) on the Lunar Exploration Committee. This was a statement of how he viewed our sister world, of how the mysteries of that world only seemed to multiply the more it was studied, including the mystery of its origin.

Like the original Rosetta Stone, which was used to determine how to translate Egyptian hieroglyphics, it was Dr. Jastrow's contention that if we could figure out these mysteries of the Moon, it might reveal much about the other celestial bodies inhabiting our solar system.

As an adjunct to this, much later, after six physical landings on the Moon had been accomplished by various Apollo astronauts, Earl Ubell, the noted science writer stated:

"...the lunar Rosetta Stone remains a mystery. The Moon is more complicated than anyone expected; it is not simply a kind of billiard ball frozen in space and time, as many scientists had believed. Few of the fundamental questions have been answered, but the Apollo rocks and recordings have spawned a score of mysteries, a few truly breath-stopping."

"Breath-stopping," "blessed coincidences," "mysterious?" Aren't scientists beginning to sound just a little too religious in their descriptions of the Moon by this point? After all, the same labels could be applied to any major religion and are often used by some, such as Catholicism. But for scientists to use such when describing attributes of our Moon is an oddity in itself.

Oddity of few craters in the *maria*. Those vast "seas" of frozen lava called *maria* are a bit of a mystery, as well. There are far fewer craters in these regions. Since craters accumulate with time, it is supposed the lava flows that created the *maria* had to have occurred after many of the craters were already formed on the Moon, and the lava flowed over them, flooding and subsequently burying them. Only more recent meteorite impacts then created the craters we see in the *maria* today.

However, this means the *maria* are far more recent in origin than many of those initial crater impacts. Yet, scientists had thought they were formed early on in the Moon's history.

What caused the Moon to belch millions of tons of lava onto its surface long after that time, after the surface had cooled and had then accumulated numerous craters from subsequent meteor impacts? Something momentous had to have occurred.

And where did the magma come from? Did the energy of the impact create it, or did it all come from a liquid core, one it isn't supposed to have had? Again, so many mysteries, so many oddities unaccounted for, even after all this time, all the study we've done of our nearest neighbor.

Strange Aristarchus Crater, the "Blue Gem" oddity. This crater has a long history of oddities. Strange lights, blue flashes, blue mists, blue glows, you name it, Aristarchus seems to have had them over the centuries. In more recent times, 1963, observations done at the Lowell Observatory reported "reddish glows" along the tops of ridges of the crater. Then, some days later, multicolored lights were reported being seen on the Moon, and by more than one observatory, thus corroborating each other that such events actually occurred.

Moreover, these observations did not occur during a sunset or sunrise on the Moon, so it was not a "trick of the lighting." However, so often are blue flashes, lights, "blue beacons," and blue pulses seen there by observers that the Aristarchus Crater has earned the nickname, "the Blue Gem."

The oddity of heavier rock on the surface of the Moon. There are three different layers of material on the Moon. There may be more, but these are the ones known so far. Oddly, the densest of these, meaning the heaviest type of rock is found on the surface of the Moon. This shouldn't be, because as we all know, denser materials, being heavier, sink.

Lighter material floats. Therefore, densest materials should be at the center of the Moon, not at the surface. That's the way it is on Earth, and should be on the Moon, too. But this is not the case. Why? Scientists don't seem to know. Oh, they theorize, but as yet, haven't come up with any substantial/adequate theory to explain this oddity.

Furthermore, the mineral content of the Moon differs markedly from the Earth in that Earth has far more iron than the Moon does. And remember in an earlier chapter we mentioned how dry the Moon's material is, compared to that of Earth's? Yet, fragments of oxidized iron have been found in lunar samples. Oxidized iron is simply iron that has rusted.

Where did the water (or hydrogen) and oxygen come from to accomplish this on a world that is supposed to be airless? And rust (oxidization) takes time, which means there had to be a supply of these gases for a considerable period to cause this rusting.

As it turns out, there is some water on the Moon after all, and that may possibly account for how iron could rust or oxidize, but it isn't in great quantities or hardly in all areas. Actual water in any detectable amounts seems to lie buried in the moon's surface, but only in the permanent shadows of some craters, such as those at the Lunar South Pole, where light never hits to heat and evaporate the frozen stuff.

Yet how water got there is something of a mystery. Moreover, how rocks in general can have a higher percentage of water than expected is yet another oddity. Asteroid or comet impacts might leave some water behind in the permanent shadows of crater walls, but this still doesn't explain or account for the higher than normally expected water content of Moon rock in general. This is an added mystery.

Chapter Conclusion. As we have noted here in this book so far, mysteries about the Moon abound. Our closest planetary neighbor, whom we humans have actually visited in person on several occasions, is full of enigmas. Suffice it to say some bizarre things appear to be going on with the Moon, and so far, we've just scratched the surface in mentioning what some of these things are.

Furthermore, the strangeness isn't just about what's going with our satellite now, but also how it even came to be there. Yet, of all the planetary bodies in our solar system (besides the Earth), this has been the most closely observed one by the most people, and for the longest period of time. And yet, mysteries about it flourish, and if anything, the sheer number of such enigmas just seems to keep growing. Oddities are the norm on the Moon, not the exception.

What does this mean? Are we just saying the Moon is a very strange place? Well, it is, but it's also apparently something else. Based on all the oddities, all the weird mysteries concerning the Moon, it just shouldn't be. At least, not the way it is.

Too much is too peculiar to all be easily accounted for when examining the Moon. Things are out of place. Things are off from the expected, what our theories tell us they should be. Everything our theories hold as valid are being challenged. This is true for the Moon's orbit, the make of its material, its isotope ratios, its water content, the fact that for a dead and airless world it behaves very much and often at times in odds with this. Moreover, we can't even seem to come up with a convincing theory of how the Moon got there! Here we are, just a little world and we have an oversized Moon, the origins for which, we can't explain!

So if nothing else, these two chapters on the oddities of the Moon do tell us something. Our Moon is distinctly unusual! But it doesn't stop there. In the next chapters, we will discuss bizarre aspects of the Moon, ones that are baffling enough to cause some reputable scientists to think the Moon may be hollow.

CHAPTER 6
Idea Of A Hollow Moon

Well, now that we've established the basic facts of the Moon, and have had a look at all the oddities, strange things involving our neighboring world, there follows the next question we must wonder about as a matter of course. That is, could the Moon actually be hollow? It sounds like an incredible question, we know, but there is some real basis for it being a fact, if only because of the oddities and some other evidence.

Yes, there are questions about that "evidence" but then there are some major questions about every theory of the Moon's origin, as well, as we've shown, but that doesn't stop countless scientists and seemingly endless television shows from propounding them as if they were fact, even now. However, the Hollow Moon Theory seems to answer more questions than it raises, unlike the other origin theories.

For instance, we're betting anyone with an interest in this subject has seen at least one television show that shows a mars-sized planet (Theia) colliding with Earth to produce the Moon. Often, this "theory" is cited more as a fact, a given, than just what it really is, and that is a theory with some real problems attached to it.

Now, let's discuss some other much more controversial theories of the Moon's origin, different ones most scientists (but not all), dismiss, or would like to dismiss out of hand.

The Spaceship Moon Theory. This is probably the first, or at least one of the first real theories where the idea is discussed the Moon may not be what it seems to be, that it may, in fact, be hollow. This theory, which is often also referred to as the Vasin-Shcherbakov Theory, postulates the Moon may not actually be a satellite of Earth, at least not a natural one.

Messrs. Michael Vasin and Alexander Shcherbakov, who at the time of the formulation of this theory were members in good standing of the Soviet Academy of Sciences, first proposed this idea in Is the Moon the Creation of Intelligence, an article they wrote in July of 1970.

They developed the theory the Moon was an unnatural thing. They said it could well be a worldlet that had been hollowed out by aliens, ones obviously having a far superior technology to ours. They went on to say the aliens may well have used such technologies to make the center of the Moon molten and then removed this liquid magma by ejecting it onto the surface of the Moon.

The result? The Moon would be a hollow shell, with a rocky and natural-looking exterior, except for those large areas of solidified magma, which we see as *maria* today.

They further proposed the inner shell would be made of metal, for added structural support. At some point after this was done, our Moon was then moved into such a nearly perfect, circular orbit around the Earth for reasons unknown.

Besides citing the *maria* as the exudate of the liquefied interior of the Moon, they also pointed to the craters on the Moon, particularly the larger ones, as another indication of their Spaceship Moon theory.

You see, despite some of the Moon's craters being truly massive in area, they are all very shallow, at least the larger ones are. If formed from meteors and asteroids colliding with the Moon, these scientists argued this would not be the case. The craters should be much deeper.

Instead, again, they're shallow and relatively flat in their centers. In some cases, the bottoms of the craters are even convex in shape, bulging slightly. They use this as further evidence the craters could not have been formed as thought by meteor impacts in the way believed by most astronomers.

Is this a credible idea? Well, it does seem on the Moon the smaller craters do have depths proportionate to their area in size. Their interiors are proportionately deep to their diameters, in other words. However, as the two scientists argued, this doesn't seem to be true of larger craters on the Moon. Why?

How does one account for this disturbing discrepancy? Well, the authors say this is so because the smaller craters were actually created by meteor impacts, which burrow their way into the surface of the Moon. However, the two Russian scientists claim this layer is only about some five miles deep.

The larger impact craters, which should have impacted more deeply, were stopped by the inner hull, the metal one supposedly manufactured by the aliens. This, the two scientists say, would account for the shallowness of the larger craters. Despite the size of the striking object, it's speed, and force, the inner "hull" of the Moon deflected it back out, thus causing the results we see only with the larger craters in the form of flat and shallow centers. So although they are the results of impacts, they weren't "allowed" to penetrate as deeply as they should, and thus the shallow interiors of the larger craters.

They have a point. If what they argue is true, it would, indeed, account for the shallowness of larger craters, versus the more proportional depths of the smaller ones. The bigger meteors simply couldn't get past the inner hull. The smaller impacts never drove that deeply into the Moon's rocky surface to reach the inner hull, so their depth is "normal."

Also part of their theory is the thickness of the inner "steel" hull. They say that below the rocky outer layer of the Moon, the metal one might then be as much as 20 miles thick. Inside of this would be an open space, which could be used for any purpose or purposes. They also say it might well contain an atmosphere.

Furthermore, both men also used the evidence of the composition of the material on the surface of the Moon. They pointed out that Titanium, Zirconium and Chromium make up a larger part of that material than on Earth, which makes it considerably different in detail from the materials on the crust of the Earth.

So as much alike as the isotopic ratio and makeup of the Moon's material to the Earth's mantle material is, there are significant differences still. The scientists went even further. They said some rocks found on the Moon date farther back than any found on Earth, itself. What does this mean? Well, it must mean the Moon would then be older than the Earth, formed before it did… or the Moon was created before the Earth was by "someone."

Also, Apollo 17 brought back some dust samples, which were composed of orange glass spherules (tiny spheres), along with fragments of other minerals. The particles are quite small and range in size from 20 microns to 45 microns. What's more, and quite differently than Apollo 11 material brought back, the orange samples were highly and unaccountably wealthy in zinc content.

What was the standard explanation for this by mainstream scientists? They say the material probably originated from volcanoes. Although, and despite a number of actual Moon landings by NASA, no volcanoes, active or extinct, have ever been discovered.

Whether any ever existed on the Moon is a matter for conjecture. So if not volcanoes, from where did this "dust" then come?

By these pieces of evidence, and others, Alexander and Michael argued the Moon might have been created before the Earth (again, citing the older age of some Moon rocks than any found on Earth), and so had a different origin.

They weren't alone in this belief. In his 1975 book Our Mysterious Moon, author Don Wilson listed a series of facts he believed acted as supporting evidence for the idea of a hollow Moon.

Nor was he alone in this. Author George H Leonard in his book Someone Else Is on the Moon, published in 1976, included a series of NASA photos purportedly showing large and artificial-looking structures on the Moon. He believed some of these structures might be huge pieces of machinery.

Do most other mainstream scientists discount this theory? Of course, they do. For one thing, they claim the disparity in the age of some rocks from the Moon versus the lesser age of those on Earth is due to tectonic activity on our planet. Rocks are "recycled" on Earth, and this accounts for the disparity. Being all recycled by now, they are simply younger.

This is a plausible idea, but is it correct? Again, we simply don't know. It's just as much a theory at the moment as the Hollow Moon Theory is. However, to date, none seem to be able to account for the orange "dust" samples and their origin, or why they should be so heavy in zinc content. Also, none seem able to account for the difference in the amount of Chromium, Titanium and Zirconium between lunar surface samples of rocks and those of rocks on Earth.

Chapter Conclusion. So, although the Spaceship Moon Theory is controversial to say the least, the fact two mainstream scientists proposed it and backed their arguments with some credible evidence must certainly be taken into consideration. Added to this, are those others who championed the idea.

CHAPTER 7

Is The Moon Really Hollow?

So now having dealt with a multitude of other oddities, all which later will figure into our theories about the Moon in this book, we now have to ask the question, could the Moon, in actual fact, be hollow? Is this even possible?

What conditions must it meet in order to be an "empty shell? What would be the major problems with such a theory? In this chapter, we intend to show there is a good possibility the Moon may just be hollow by answering these questions.

How does one go about doing this? Well, the best way is, of course, by finding more supporting evidence for the theory the Spaceship Moon may be true, or at least in some form of variation of it. As mentioned, evidence shouldn't hinge on just one source alone, but as many as possible. To use a metaphor, if enough "One-Way" arrow signs are posted on a street, then the street is probably "one-way." Right?

The same holds true for theories. Find enough evidence from a variety of sources to support a theory and the theory just may be true. How true? Well, if we do it to the level of our "one-way" sign example, just ask yourself: Would you drive down that street the wrong way and ignore all those warning signs? Probably not, unless you were terribly intoxicated at the time.

No. You wouldn't chance it. That's how "true" you think the idea of those posted signs being right is. Although maybe not absolutely certain, you feel the likelihood of it being true so great, you don't wish to challenge it by driving the wrong way. So for you, the theory is valid enough that it alters your behavior and your plans as to which way you are going to drive.

We want to do this with the Hollow Moon Theory, to provide enough sign posts to make you think the idea is, or least could well be, possible. Again, the best way to do this is to try to find evidence from different sources, different "disciplines."

This means we shouldn't just rely on the originators of the Hollow Moon Theory, Messrs. Vasin and Shcherbakov, and the evidence they cite for it, because in our estimation, that simply isn't quite enough.

We should try to find other corroborating sources of evidence, as well. The more "legs" we provide as sources of evidence, the more we build our case, the more valid the theory then becomes and can stand on its own. We've already started on doing this by pointing out all those oddities of the Moon's origin and its physical, as well as orbital characteristics. Again, these we will tie in later.

First, as shown in the prior chapter, some of the conditions for a hollow Moon have already been met by the evidence cited in the Spaceship Moon Theory by Michael Vasin and Alexander Shcherbakov. To recap, the main points were:

1. We have the massive but shallow craters, as opposed to smaller ones that are as deep as they should be, proportional to their area of circumference, while the larger ones are not. This could be indicative of a harder substrate that blocked further penetration of the bigger and faster meteors. This being the 20-mile-thick inner shell (give or take a few miles) Messrs. Vasin and Shcherbakov talk about in their theory.

2. We have the *maria* as possible exudate, the molten rock "they" (the aliens) might have melted and then forced or pumped up onto the lunar surface to create a hollow interior. Anyone looking at the Moon at night can clearly see these vast dark patches of relatively flat and frozen lava flows. Otherwise, how to account for them? If there are no volcanoes, there shouldn't be any magma under normal circumstances, either. No plate tectonics, no geothermal activity—no magma. It's as simple as that. So where did the mares come from? Scientists seem unsure otherwise.

3. The Moon's age is still in question. If it does predate the Earth that would tell us the Moon didn't form along with the Earth, and so is from "somewhere else." The age of certain rocks from the Moon do clearly date farther back in time than any found on Earth.

Along with these pieces of evidence, we have all those oddities we spoke of earlier, which we will now elaborate on here, examine in more detail as promised:

1. As mentioned earlier, mineral make-up of materials on the surface of the Moon have oddly high quantities of Titanium and Zinc, which similar surface materials on Earth do not, Titanium definitely being one of the rarer elements here. This would indicate although the oxygen-isotope ratios match surface material on the Moon to surface material on the Earth, that something else was going on there, something big, as well, to account for these differences.

No current theories of the Moon yet account for this problem at all, this major discrepancy. However, if the Moon were an artificial product, had undergone major alterations, this could account for this difference.

2. The "orange dust" seems to have come from "somewhere else," purportedly volcanoes on the Moon. However, and despite numerous photographs of the lunar surface, besides actual manned, lunar landings and human explorations, as well as robotic ones, no volcanoes have been found, either active or dormant. So from where did this "volcanic" dust come?

Again, no other current theories of the Moon seem to account for this. However, if someone were "blowing out" vast amounts of the interior in a way similar to volcanoes, this would account for the orange spheres.

3. The origin theories of the Moon all have some major problems with them, big drawbacks that as of the date of this book, have not been accounted for in any realistic or cogent way. This is why various reputable scientists, as recently as 2010-2011, are still propagating new theories. Each of the main theories, including the planetary impact theory, still leaves big questions unresolved. Yet, if the moon here hollow, artificially created and/or altered, this would answer all these questions/oddities.

4. And remember the far side of the Moon. The crust is thicker there than the nearer side. The Impact Theory really stretches to account for this. If one uses the Principle of Occam's Razor here, so unwieldy is the theory at this point, that some scientists and with good reason we feel, are proposing others, such as the Georeactor Theory. However, if the interior were being pumped out as molten magma, and this wasn't evenly distributed, this could account for the differences in thickness between the two sides.

5. The orbit of the Moon is almost perfectly circular, and this is so unlikely as to make one think the orbit is an artificial one, with someone having deliberately entered the Moon into such a type of orbit. Again, orbits are just not normally circular. They are elliptical. So something has to "make" a planet or Moon take up a circular orbit. For the Moon to have such a one is an incredible oddity in itself and would have required real precision to achieve. So is this really just by chance, a coincidence. The number of coincidences at this point with regard to the Moon do act to stretch one's credulity.

6. By all accounts, the Moon should have a wobble to it, but strangely, it doesn't. Somehow, something has compensated for a wobble that should definitely be there. If the gravitational center is off because of the Earth's gravitational influence, something must be correcting or have corrected for this offset (and resulting wobble) at some point in the past. After all, even the Earth has a wobble, which can start and stop, but is usually there.

To date, no wobble of the Moon has ever been seen. If the Moon is hollow, that would account for this state of affairs. "Something" in the interior could be offset, thus correcting for any such possible wobble.

7. As mentioned earlier, the Moon rings like a (hollow) bell when struck or impacted, as with the crashing of the lunar landers back onto its surface. It does this for hours, which greatly surprised scientists, and it is a phenomenon for which they can't account. Their theories of the Moon's structure don't explain this. However, if the Moon were hollow, this would account for such a phenomenon. Being hollow like a bell, it would tend to "ring" or "resonate" like a bell.

Furthermore, seismic waves seem to be deflected away from the core of the Moon, and again, scientists don't understand why, can't comprehend the cause of this phenomenon. Once more, current theories about the core can't account for this effect.

However, if the Moon had a hollow core, this would certainly result in such an outcome, for there would be nothing for the seismic waves to travel through at the core, not in an open space. They would then be deflected "around" the empty core. This seems to be what is actually happening.

8. The surface material of the Moon is unusually hard, so hard in fact; astronauts had big problems drilling for samples. If the Moon was artificially altered to better withstand meteor impacts, this would account for such an unusual "hardness." Simply put, it was "made that way."

9. Frequent moonquakes, despite there being supposedly no tectonic activity on the Moon, also cannot now be accounted for very well with current theories of the Moon's internal structure. Tidal influences could possibly account for these, as mentioned, but the quakes don't seem to occur in sequence with the peak of such tidal influences, as they should have to do, but occur rather randomly. This, they should definitely not do under such circumstances and not if the theory of tidal causes is correct.

So just what is causing them? Could it be some sort of internal activity that isn't tectonic related at all, something aliens might be doing "in there" that is shaking the shell of the Moon?

10. Do you remember our earlier references to transient lunar events? A steady stream of ancient and more recent sightings of strange events have, and continue even now, to occur on the Moon, including "pulses of light," "beacons," "flashes," "streaks," "beams," "tracks," etc. Again, so many of these sightings are there, NASA has coined the term of Transient Lunar Phenomena for them.

What could account for so many different types of events as these on a supposedly dead world? If aliens did inhabit the interior of the Moon, and were coming and going in space-going vessels, or occasionally (for whatever reason(s)) making excursions out on the surface, perhaps even with bases there, then this would account for all such strange "transient lunar phenomena." In fact, it is the only explanation that seems to cover all types of such phenomena, since no other theory can account for all the diverse types of anomalous events seen on the Moon over the centuries. Just that one theory does, that the Moon is hollow and may have inhabitants.

11. The Gravitational field of the Moon is strongest in patches over the *maria*. The gravitational field of the Moon varies, even as it does somewhat on Earth, depending on areas of higher density. NASA has shown the Moon's gravitational field is "lumpy," that is, it's stronger in some areas than others.

Oddly, because the higher gravitational areas seem to center over the *maria*, we do have a very reasonable explanation for this with the Hollow Moon Theory.

If those seas are composed of congealed core material, having been pumped out from the center of the Moon, then the material from the core would naturally have been denser than material at the surface. Heavy stuff sinks toward the center, remember? And if pumped out onto the surface, this would increase its influence on the gravitational field of the Moon in those areas, making it stronger.

Even as mountains on Earth influence the local power of the gravitational field near them, so would mountains on the Moon, However, why would relatively flat areas of frozen lava flows have such an effect, unless the material which makes them up is unusually dense, meaning, perhaps, being core material?

Chapter Conclusion. So we aren't just talking about just a few oddities here, but many and major ones, at that. What's more, combined with the claims of the two Russian scientists, something far stranger, far more bizarre does seem to be a distinct possibility. Again, perhaps it's because the Moon may be hollow.

Even if the Moon isn't, at the very least, something very weird is going on with our neighbor, something for which no current theories can account. And if it isn't hollow, then how do we explain all these things, these "oddities?" At present, scientists simply can't, not in any other way.

However, if the Moon had been created artificially or altered and then placed in orbit around our world, many or all of these questions would be answered. The Hollow Moon theory seems to answer more questions than any other theory of the Moon's origin we have at present. In short, it seems the best fit as an explanation for the origin of our Moon precisely because it answers the most questions.

CHAPTER 8

More Information About A Hollow Moon

Before we go further, please note at this point and it is very important to note, we are not talking about Earth being hollow, but rather the Moon. We make no claims whatsoever as to whether the Earth is hollow or not. We suspect strongly it isn't. Evidence in that regard seems to be overwhelming it is not. It may have large caverns, but these would hardly constitute or be anywhere near on the order of being able to call the Earth "hollow."

However, the Moon could well be. Whether this is in the form of the entire center of our Moon being empty or just massive caverns within its interior, we can't be certain. If the caverns are extensive enough, they could result in that "hollow ringing" that occurs when any object strikes the lunar surface.

So is the Moon actually hollow?

Well, here is some more interesting information in further support of such an idea. We're betting most people didn't even realize this. For instance:

The Moon isn't dense enough. The average mean density of our nearest neighbor is 3.34 grams per cubic centimeter. This is low, very low, and only about three and a third times the density of water! How can this be?

Unlike the Moon, the average mean density of the Earth works out to about 5.5 times that of water, so its density is considerably higher than our neighbor. This, despite the fact the Moon is supposed to be composed of material from Earth and so should have the same density? What can account for this major inconsistency?

This presents scientists with a major problem, this disparity in densities between us and our sister world. Furthermore, there are very few ways the Moon could be as large as it is, and have such a low density.

Dr. Harold Urey, a Nobel Prize winning chemist, made the observation that the disparity in densities between our two worlds, meaning the much lower density of the Moon compare to the Earth, might be accounted for by the Moon having "simply a cavity."

Red flag here! A Nobel Prize winner saying the moon might be hollow?

Another noted scientist, Dr. Farouk El Baz, went even further in his statements and implications, when he said:

"There are many undiscovered caverns suspected to exist beneath the surface of the Moon. Several experiments have been flown to the Moon to see if there actually were such caverns."

Red flag again! If the moon has caverns of enough size to change its overall density, so that it is far less than Earth's, those caverns must be of truly massive proportions, e.g., a hollow Moon, basically?

To date, the findings of such missions and experiments have not yet been made available. As seems to be the usual case these days with such matters, one has to ask why this hasn't happened. Why hasn't the general public had access to these results?

And of course, the usual response to such questions seems to be no answer at all. A sort of stonewalling mentality seems to be the order of the day when it comes to certain topics, ones that NASA seems simply to refuse to respond to in any realistic way.

However, even Dr. Gordon MacDonald, a NASA scientist, declared that:

"If the astronomical data are reduced, it is found that the data require that the interior of the Moon is more like a hollow than a homogeneous sphere."

Red flag yet again! Another scientist, a NASA one this time, daring to say the Moon may be hollow? Nor is he alone in this determination.

Much later, Dr. Sean Solomon stated that:

"...the Lunar Orbiter experiments vastly improved our knowledge of the Moon's gravitational field...indicating the frightening possibility that the Moon might be hollow."

Red flag yet one more time! Yet another NASA scientist making the claim the Moon might be hollow? Really?

Werner von Braun, called the Father of American Rocketry by many, stated in Popular Science in a 1970 article, How Apollo 13 Will Probe the Moon's Interior. He discussed the idea that when the main section of the Apollo 12 was allowed to impact the Moon that,

"The astounding result of that crash: The Moon rang like a bell for nearly an hour, indicating some strange and unearthly underground structure."

Dr. Wernher von Braun was the Director at NASA for quite a while.

Could this "hollowness" have somehow come about naturally? Well, this just doesn't seem very likely at all. Why? Well as the noted (famous) scientist, the host of the original PBS TV series, ***Cosmos,*** Carl Sagan, once remarked in his Intelligent Life in the Universe treatise:

"A natural satellite cannot be a hollow object."

So by sheer logic, if the Moon is hollow, then according to no less than Carl Sagan, it cannot be a natural satellite. He is saying this, not us.

All these comments and statements by renowned astronomers and cosmologists must lend great credence to the idea of a hollow Moon, especially given all the above peculiarities of the Moon, and how the satellite having been hollowed out seems best to explain them.

And one should remember that not only do they theorize the idea of the Moon having a hollow center to explain the density disparity, but as Carl Sagan put it so succinctly, it couldn't have come about that way through any "natural" means. That only leaves the "unnatural," doesn't it, by sheer default?

Chapter Conclusion. But after all is said and done is the Moon we see in our night skies really just an empty shell? Does all this data supply the necessary information to confirm such an idea? In other words, can we know for sure? Well, there are no absolutes, as most of us have found out at some point in our lives, but that doesn't mean we can't attempt to go even further to try to find the answers. This much, we can do.

CHAPTER 9
Different Legs To Stand On

There is even more evidence we can draw on to try to find the truth of the Hollow Moon Theory, if it is really so. Remember those different "legs," the different types of evidence, from different sources we talked about? When trying to supply "legs" to support a theory, such different sources of evidence can act as powerful corroboration for such an idea, giving it (almost literally) "more legs to stand on." Moreover, there is such evidence. We have it.

For example, NASA, it seems, has a history of people who have stepped outside of official bounds and made some extraordinary claims. These people include those who worked directly for NASA in positions of trust, as well as people who worked as security-cleared contractors, and even as astronauts actively involved in the NASA space missions. Even top-level administrators from NASA are involved.

There is something else, as well. There are photographs of strange things on the lunar surface, along with even some video, and even recorded vocal broadcasts of astronauts, regarding bizarre occurrences in space and on lunar missions.

Photographic Evidence For Alien Structures On The Moon? Let's cut to the chase here. Is there actual photographic evidence for alien structures on the Moon? In our opinion, the answer would appear to be yes.

Over the decades, pictures of strange things on the Moon keep cropping up. These photographs come from NASA, itself. And although they deny these are photographs of actual structures, and use various explanations for them, such as "outgassing," if one looks at the actual photos, these sorts of justifications just don't seem to work, at least they don't or us. And we don't think they do for anyone who really examines the pictures. Mind you, we're not talking about photos from dubious sources, ones that may have been retouched or altered, but original NASA photos from NASA. Case in point:

The Shard. In a photograph, Lunar Orbiter frame LO-III-84-M is a somewhat over exposed picture. Photographed from about 250 miles away, the picture is of an object that has since become known simply as the "shard."

This is a rather curious photograph. A closer examination of the picture, and using some enhancement, clearly shows that whatever this is, it is casting a shadow onto the lunar surface, and the shadow is in the right direction, given the origin of the lighting in the photograph. This means that it probably is actually something on the Moon and not just an optical illusion. Illusions don't cast shadows. Just what is it? Nobody seems to be sure.

However, because of the poor quality of this photograph and others similar to it, NASA puts the image down to being nothing more than an outgassing, or an anomaly of some sort, perhaps a flaw in the film.

Yet, the shadow being in line with the lighting in the photo, rather than with the grain of the film, makes such a supposition far less likely. Again, an "anomaly," a flaw in the film doesn't cast a shadow. Moreover, on a dead world with no atmosphere at all to speak of, where is this "outgassing" supposedly coming from?

The Tower. This is an object situated just behind the shard. If it is an actual structure, and not just another abnormality, then it stands some seven miles in height! As outlandish as such a thing would seem to be, and it is something we simply can't accomplish on Earth, because of our heavier gravity making the engineering of such structures impossible, such would be conceivable on the Moon.

With only one-sixth the gravity of Earth, on the Moon, such an engineering feat is feasible. With enhancements, the tower shows an internal "cellular" structure. The shard, too, using similar enhancements, shows the same thing.

Of course, because of the poor quality of the photograph, NASA has concluded that if this isn't just a flaw in the development of the picture, then perhaps it is another outgassing. The question is an outgassing of what? Again, the Moon is supposed to be a dead world, with many scientists believing the core has to be solid, and so there being no tectonic or volcanic activity. Moreover, if it isn't an outgassing and just a flaw in the film, then it is incredible NASA would use such low-grade, poor quality of film for such expensive missions to have so many flaws. This would seem to be unlikely.

What's more, astronauts found no sign of geysers, vents, or anything that might cause or allow for such outgassing. Neither do high-resolution photographs of the Moon's surface, taken since then, show anything of this nature.

Furthermore, there aren't the usual side effects of such a thing, as is any sort of blotchiness, speckling, or bespattered areas or regions that one would normally associate with such an outgassing. Under enhancement, the object looks solid, as if "weathered" by meteor strikes over a long period of time.

And unlike the photograph of the shard, other pictures taken years later by other missions also show the tower. This would make it seem all the more likely the shard was a real object, as well, and not just an anomaly or a "gas."

Ukert Crater. Now, with regard to one stranger feature, the Ukert Crater, we have some weird things going on there, as well. Low resolution photographs of the crater, taken by the Clementine Mission, (more correctly known as Clementine the Deep Space

Program Science Experiment (DSPSE)), show a very triangular-looking crater and it does not conform to the normal shapes of craters (circular) at all. An argument has been proposed this is the result of a partial collapse of the wall encircling the crater, but no such collapsed crater walls resemble this shape anywhere else on the Moon.

So why here, we have to wonder? Again why is this also in the peculiar area noted for so many other "anomalies?" Furthermore and very puzzling to us is why high resolution pictures of the crater are "blacked out" on all the various Clementine websites. They have been deliberately made unavailable.

This, in itself, is not just highly curious, but very intriguing, as well. And let's face it, suspicious. Is someone hiding something by doing this? Do the higher resolution versions of the photographs show something too clearly, something the government doesn't want the public to know about?

The Castle. From the photograph, AS10-32-4822, taken on an Apollo mission, one can see a very strange structure. In the photograph, which is unenhanced by the way, one can clearly see sections composing the structure. This object is floating approximately around three miles above the lunar surface!

Photographic anomalies simply don't explain this away, nor does the concept of outgassing. So just what is it? Well, it clearly looks artificial. Also, it's huge. Whatever it is, it does not seem to be manmade, not in the human sense of the term. Subsequent pictures show the Castle at different angles, which adds to the idea that this is a real, three-dimensional object, and not just some weird photographic illusion.

There is something else about these photographs, as well. Whatever this thing is, the Castle, it looks entirely artificial, and hardly natural in either shape or design. This is no asteroid somehow magically floating a few miles above the surface of the Moon. And there's more. If one looks closely at the shape and design of the Castle, one notices marked similarities to the shard and tower in its design.

"Los Angeles." Next we come to a photograph referred to as Frame AS10-32-4822. This is an area of the Moon the researcher, Richard Hoagland, referred to as "Los Angeles." (When one looks at it, there is a resemblance to the L.A. Basin, just without the smog.) And oddly, this is a region of the Moon approximately the size of the Los Angeles Basin in area.

The image is another bizarre one. Why? Well, because there is more than just one "oddity" about this photograph. First, there is the matter of those "city blocks" that seem so prevalent in this peculiar area. There is what can only be described as rectangular shapes laid out in a sort of grid pattern. Please go to:

http://www.bibliotecapleyades.net/luna/esp_luna_26.htm to see photos of this, as well as the other objects.

These rectangular shapes do not appear to be "natural." The situation of them, their layout on the lunar surface, bears a close resemblance to aerial photographs of ruins of ancient cities here on Earth, in that the shapes repeat, and rather resemble city blocks, as in being laid out in a repeating pattern, an artificial way.

Paperclip. Then there is the matter of the "paperclip," as Mr. Hoagland calls it. He thinks it may be a type of antenna, since the thing resembles some of those on Earth in its shape. Furthermore, the "paperclip" appears to be at the top of a long supporting pole. Whatever the paperclip actually is, it does not appear to be a natural feature of the Moon at all. What's more, given the dimensions of the area and its relative size in the picture to those dimensions, the paperclip is very large, huge indeed, on the order of a tall building as in, say, New York.

Crystal Palace. Then there is also the so-called "Crystal Palace," (a nickname given to the object by Mr. Hoagland). This would appear to be a mammoth structure, being the equivalent of a number of miles in circumference. Its appearance is very similar to that of glass or some other such transparent material, and is far more reflective than the surrounding area of the Moon there.

Mr. Hoagland uses the term "arcology" to describe it, as well, since it seems the "Crystal Palace" may have been a domed structure of some sort, a vast one, and now seemingly in ruins. (Could meteorite impacts over the ages be the cause of this ruined state?)

Now, if all these objects appear fuzzy, hazy, or questionably indistinct to you, there is yet one more oddity about this same region. If you look at the lower right portion of the photograph of the Los Angeles Basin, strange grooves or lines show on the lunar surface. These progress in straight lines and then suddenly take very sharp, right-angle turns. This is not a natural consequence of erosion. First, erosion doesn't travel in straight lines and make right-angle, 90 degree turns.

Then, too, secondly, there is no erosion on the Moon. No atmosphere, so no rain, so no water at all (or anything else) that could cause erosion.

So these lines or "grooves" certainly do not appear to be natural features. If they were the result of some sort of liquid erosion (possibly lava, for instance?), again, one does not see such straight lines, or such sharp right angles. Liquids do not flow in such a pattern under most circumstances, unless artificially made to do so.

So just what are these lines or grooves? They are quite clear in the photograph, quite distinct, and quite weird.

Lunar Bridge. John J. O'Neill, long before humans walked on the Moon, on July 29, 1953, declared he had observed what he called a bridge, apparently some twelve miles in length, spanning the Mare Crisium Crater. Please go to:

https://www.google.com/search?q=lunar+bridge+on+moon+john+j.+o%27neill&client=firefox-a&hs=wO6&rls=org.mozilla:en-

US:official&channel=sb&tbm=isch&tbo=u&source=univ&sa=X&ei=mbs-U9eKJInksASYt4LgCQ&ved=0CDAQsAQ&biw=1024&bih=590

to see photos of this. And yes, some NASA scientists like to call it an "illusion," but there is a problem with that idea.

You see, another noted astronomer, Dr. H.P. Wilkins, corroborated that the "bridge" did actually seem to be there. However, in more recent photographs taken by NASA of the area, the "bridge" appears to have vanished. However, when it was still there, Wilkins made a very telling statement. Quote:

"It looks artificial. It's almost incredible that such a thing could have been formed in the first instance, or if it was formed, could have lasted during the ages in which the Moon has been in existence."

We find this last item, the Lunar Bridge, particularly odd. Telescopes were very good by 1953. Additionally, these were two well-respected astronomers, only distantly connected as professional colleagues, so the idea they may have been colluding in a hoax is patently absurd.

One spies a "bridge," which later the other astronomer then verifies. What exactly were they both seeing? Was it some sort of temporary structure, of did our "shadowy government," which we will also discuss later on, remove images of the structure from all later photographs taken of the region?

Strange structures "nuked" on the Moon? Now this is very offbeat, because it appears to have been a mistake on the part of NASA in that these photographs apparently weren't intended to be shown. An interviewer, perhaps accidentally or possibly on purpose, took photographs of pictures lying on a table during an interview with two of the researchers at the AMES facilities, Dr. Kim Ennico, and Anthony Colaprete.

So again, the photographs lying on the table were never meant to be seen by the public, at least not on the part of the researchers, apparently, for they appear nowhere else, and seem to have been overlooked by the interviewees. In other words, they just happened to be there and were unnoticed by their owners.

In the one photograph with the image of one of the researcher's arms resting on it, one can clearly see a rectangular structure that by no stretch of the imagination could be called "natural." Please go to: http://www.ancient-code.com/alien-moon-base-in-official-nasa-images/ to see an image of this. Oddly, this is the same area of the Moon, scientists deliberately allowed the mission-finished spacecraft (Centaur) to impact on the Moon.

Ostensibly, this was just to raise a cloud of debris, which could then undergo spectroscopic analysis, primarily to search for water content, among other things. Was the purpose of the impact really something else entirely? Was it to obliterate evidence of the structure, an ancient alien ruin, instead? More of this sort of thing can be seen at the website listed under "References" at the end of this book.

Circular base on the Moon. Then there is the photo, Frame AS15-87-11697 taken on an Apollo mission which shows a circular "base" on the Moon, with outlying structures, and even some sort of a spoke-like object radiating out from the central tower. The shadow of the tower at the center is in line with shadows of all the craters in the photograph. What's more, this is an official NASA photo and can be found displayed on their website.

Furthermore, NASA removed the high-resolution versions from its site, so they now have only the lower resolution one, but it is still very clear, even so. However, the original high resolution picture can be found at a private website, where it was posted before the high resolution original was removed from NASA's main site.

We wanted you to be able to go to the original sites and see both versions of the photo for yourself, if you choose. The original photo, the lower resolution one, can be found at:

http://www.lpi.usra.edu/resources/apollo/frame/?AS15-87-11697

This website also gives pertinent information with regard to the photo, type of camera used, lunar longitude and latitude, etc. For the higher resolution version of the photo, please go to:

http://keithlaney.net/ApolloOrbitalimages/AS15/h/AS15-87-11697.jpg

This way, you can judge for yourself if you think this is a natural or artificial structure(s).

Also, Ken Johnston and his fellow researcher, Richard Hoagland, have made public several rather astonishing things. In Secret History of NASA, they claim the first astronaut missions to visit the Moon photographed what they believed to be ruins on the Moon. Subsequently, the photographs of these ruins and structures were ordered by NASA to be destroyed.

This order was given to the then-manager of the Data and Photo Control Department, Mr. Johnston, who instead of doing as ordered, gave the information to non-NASA sources.

Thirteen "orbs" erupt from the Moon. In September, 2012, a noted astronomer released footage that on the face of it seems to *support the idea the Moon may be hollow. This is a direct quote:*

"While filming the Moon on September the 15th 2012 with my telescope and Canon EOS 600D I spotted 13 orbs probably starting from a secret alien moonbase." [Original video at: [http://youtu.be/1XsYlI-q0hk]

So one can readily see when it comes to photographic evidence there seems to be a lot of it. How reliable are these photos? Well, we made it a point here for this book to rely on NASA's own images, with almost all being from their own websites. So, you must judge the credibility of such photographs for yourself. And in the process, you'll be judging NASA's credibility, as well.

There are more photos, as well, many more, but we chose these as being the representative ones, the most reliable to include here, simply because of their source. However, if you use some of the links at the end of this book and follow them, you can see and judge some of the other available pictures for yourself. And of course, we are wary of sources outside of NASA because these days, photographs can be so easily altered. Again, this is why we relied here principally on NASA's own pictures from their official sites.

Finally, do remember one more thing. If some of the photos seem "fuzzy," and indeterminate, this is because the only versions still available are low-resolution ones. NASA, for some reason, either has "blacked out" the higher resolution versions or removed them entirely in many cases.

Chapter Conclusion. So as always in this book, one must ask the question, why? Why did they do this, leave only the lowest resolution versions of such photos available to the public? Are they, in fact, trying to hide something by doing such a thing? Otherwise, why not make the much higher resolution photos available otherwise?

They are all by law in the public domain… supposedly. They did appear originally, but then when various members of the public and media started noticing strange things in some of those pictures, suddenly, the higher-resolutions ones were no longer available. Just why is this? To date, we have no answer to this question from NASA. However, it does make one suspicious. How cold it not? If there is nothing "there" to be seen, why not just post them and be done with it?

CHAPTER 10

Evidence Of Aliens From Astronauts

One of the things we also need to justify is the idea the ruined structures and/or still active bases on the Moon are of alien origin, and not the result of human endeavors, either past or present, somehow. Although this is unlikely, given the history of our own civilization and current technological capabilities, nevertheless, it is something that has to be considered, just to cover all eventualities in this regard.

Is it possible that this could be so? Yes, remotely possible. Very remotely possible humans might somehow have accomplished these feats at some point in the ancient past.

But if so, which solution should we go with, that humans in the past had achieved such capabilities (somehow, someway), and then lost them, or that aliens have accomplished these wonders?

Well, we rely on the principle most scientists like to cite whenever choosing the most likely answer to a theory that has more than one solution. This principle is the Principle of Occam's Razor. In the original Latin, is says:

"entia non sunt multiplicanda praeter necessitatem,

Or from the Latin into English, literally meaning: *"entities must not be multiplied beyond necessity."*—Webster's English Dictionary

Scientists translate it to mean: *"given more than one explanation, all other things being equal, the simplest is usually the correct one."*

So if we compare the two possible solutions, even now we have to admit we have no such technological capabilities as to hollow out a moon of such size. Also, historically, we have no evidence we ever had such capabilities in the past, or of building such structures on the Moon.

The simpler answer, if one goes by the Principle of Occam's Razor, is that "someone," who would most likely be aliens, accomplished these feats. However, this would only work if **(1)** aliens actually exist, and **(2)** if they seem to have an inordinate interest in our Moon.

There does seem to be a good deal of evidence this is the actual case, that aliens, in fact, are the builders of these structures and are the engineers of a hollow Moon. This would appear so (based on the state of some of the structures in the photos) to have been done far in the past, although some such constructions may still be occupied even now, if not at least, the interior of the Moon, itself.

What evidence do have for this? Well, we've already mentioned quite a number of NASA photographs and given their source sites. Now let's start with what we feel is the most reliable of other types of evidence, this being evidence that comes from various astronauts, themselves.

After all, who is more reliable in such a capacity as witnesses than our absolutely most highly trained, most trusted individuals in our own NASA space program, those who have not only conquered space for us, but landed on the surface of the Moon, as well?

Following is a list of just some of these astronauts, and their interactions with UFOs/aliens, here on Earth, in space, and on the Moon:

Astronaut Scott Carpenter. *"At no time when the astronauts were in space were they alone. There was a constant surveillance by UFOs."*

This is a very famous or perhaps infamous quotation made by the Astronaut, Scott Carpenter. Sadly, this great American recently died at the age of 88, in October of 2013. However, perhaps his "truth still marches on."

We say this, because as an astronaut, Scott Carpenter had a long and illustrious career. In 1962, he was only the second American astronaut to circle the Earth, and his was not an easy flight, but one fraught with major problems, including even the splashdown of his capsule.

Yet, the man made the above statement and apparently meant every word of it, even unto his dying day. He was convinced that at all times when astronauts were in space, whether in orbit around the Earth or going to the Moon, they were being observed by UFOs of an unknown origin. Meaning of alien origin, since we know of no one on Earth with the nearly the capabilities of such craft. He bases this on his own experiences in this regard, and things related to him by fellow astronauts.

If one of our own trusted and revered astronauts felt there was such a presence always observing our people in space and on the Moon, then it follows logically such beings could well be the ones who have bases on or inside the Moon. They may well be the originators of our "Hollow Moon."

Major Gordon Cooper. Here is an astronaut with a long connection to UFOs. First, in 1951, as a pilot in Germany flying an F-86 jet he spotted UFOs. He described them as being "metallic" in appearance, and being "saucer-shaped." Later, he added he had seen such vehicles over a span of two days, and they had seemed to be in various sizes. He also said they flew in "formation," travelling toward the west.

This last was of real significance at the time, since he was based in Western Germany, before the country was reunified with its eastern portion, which at the time was still under Communist and Soviet Russian control. So there were strong Cold War aspects involved and this is why his statements garnered even greater attention at the time than they might otherwise have.

Those in the West, were fearful the "saucers" might have been of Russian origin, but of course, the Russians had no such capabilities or anything like them, and still don't to this day. Neither do we. In fact, no one on Earth, then or now, had or has such capabilities.

But his involvement with UFOs didn't end there. Cooper later became an astronaut, and flew the last mission as a single astronaut of the Mercury program, circling the Earth for 22 consecutive orbits. It was on the last circuit, while being tracked by an Australian station located near Perth in Western Australia, that Astronaut Cooper encountered a UFO.

Major Gordon Cooper described it as a green glowing object that rapidly advanced toward his Mercury capsule, closing in on him. The significance of the Australian tracking station here is it confirmed an object on its radar screens. What does this mean? Well, it simply proves this wasn't an illusion or hallucination on the part of Major Gordon Cooper, but something real. "Somebody" flying something incredible, was in space with him. Ground radar had tracked it.

When he subsequently appeared at the United Nations to give testimony, he said, and this is a direct quote:

"I believe that these extra-terrestrial vehicles and their crews are visiting this planet from other planets."

And significantly, upon landing and recovery of him and his capsule, reporters had been informed in advance they were not allowed to ask anything pertaining to his sighting of the UFO. Although while in space his statements about it had been publicly broadcast, that subject, apparently, was off limits to the public upon his return. Nothing more was ever publicly said about the incident by NASA. It simply ceased to exist as something that had happened, or rather from their desired point of view… hadn't.

Much later, J. L. Ferrando, in a recorded interview with Astronaut Cooper, said the major had told him he had even once seen a landing site of a UFO, one that was still engulfed in flames, so recent had been the landing, and that Major Cooper had evidence, as well, of beings that had exited the vehicle. According to Mr. Ferrando, it was Cooper's assertion there was evidence for the aliens having made a foray about the area, apparently to research aspects of the region.

Furthermore, again according to Mr. Ferrando, Astronaut Cooper went on to say the following:

"For many years I have lived with a secret, in a secrecy imposed on all specialists in astronautics. I can now reveal that every day, in the USA, our radar instruments capture objects of form and composition unknown to us. And there are thousands of witness reports and a quantity of documents to prove this, but nobody wants to make them public."

So here is yet another astronaut, a brave, intelligent, and resourceful man, one made of "the right stuff," and trusted by NASA to man a space capsule by himself. It is hard to imagine NASA felt he had any shortcomings in reliability in any way, mentally or physically, such was the rigid standards and testing of the agency. Therefore, one would have to consider him a very reliable witness extremely so, for seeing a UFO in space, especially with the added evidence of the ground tracking station's radar to supplement such a statement.

Military Pilot, Major Robert White. Major Robert White, a forerunner of American astronauts, was a pilot of the high-flying spy jet, the X-15. July 17, 1962, he spotted a UFO while flying at an altitude of 58 miles (approximately). To quote Major White, he said:

"I have no idea what it could be. It was grayish in color and about thirty to forty feet away."

Later, *Time Magazine* reported in an article that he also said:

"There are things out there! There absolutely is!"

So it would seem Major White is an adherent of the existence of UFOs and aliens. They are not only in our skies, but in space, as well, if one is to believe him.

NASA Pilot Joseph Walker. A pilot for NASA, Joseph Walker said NASA had given him the assignment of spotting UFOs while performing flights in his spy plane, an X-15. He said he had taken film of a number of UFOs and that this took place on his flight to an altitude of 50 miles, which broke the records at the time. This took place in April of 1962.

The following month, on May 11, he made the statement about having seen and filmed the alien vessels. This wasn't the first time he had done this. Once before he claimed he had filmed such strange vehicles. Although he refused to make any conjectures about what he had seen, he was adamant that he had seen and filmed them.

Oddly, NASA never released any of those movies to the general public. To this day, they have not been seen by any, but a select few, it seems.

Again, and dating from the earliest days of NASA, we have one of "their own," a highly respected and brave pilot, who makes the clear statement he saw and filmed UFOs. If skeptics need a track record of such things to make them believe UFOs exist, are in our skies and space, then by this point they should have a sufficient one. But there are more.

Astronaut Ed White. Ed White, the first astronaut to take a spacewalk, was on a Gemini mission. While circling the Earth, Ed spied a metallic object. There were protrusions jutting from the vehicle, so this wasn't a typical "saucer" UFO.

Astronaut James McDivitt. White's co-astronaut on the mission, James, took photographs of the UFO. Alas, these, as with so many others, to this day have been withheld from the general public by NASA. At this point, even the most ardent anti-conspiracy advocates must begin to wonder why this constant withholding of photos by NASA. If they've nothing to hide, then why aren't they releasing all of these pictures? As one newspaper in its tagline puts it, "enquiring minds want to know."

Astronauts Frank Borman and Astronaut James Lovell. At the end of 1965, these two astronauts were performing a Gemini mission when they witnessed a UFO. This took place on only their second orbit of Earth. When Astronaut Borman radioed in what he was seeing, Mission Control at Cape Kennedy questioned the validity of his observations, and pointedly wondered if what Borman was seeing was their own booster rocket.

Borman countered this condescending question by saying the booster was in sight, but what he was viewing was not the booster. Although we have no pictures of this event (at least, none that were publicly released), the transcript is public.

In it, Borman clearly states that it is (1) not the booster he and Lovell are viewing, (2) it is an unidentified object (and he was a trained observer, so for him not to be able to identify it, tells us something), and (3) there was more than one object. Another important point here; both astronauts saw these "bogeys." Furthermore, NASA has not publicly commented to any extent on this sighting, had almost nothing to say about it at all. Why?

Astronaut Eugene Cernan. Having headed the Apollo 17 Lunar Mission, Cernan later publicly stated in the Los Angeles Times (1973) that he thought UFOs were *"somebody else"* and from *"some other civilization."* Notice, he did not say some other country.

Now this is pretty telling, because it is as much the fact he didn't deny their existence, as well as saying what he thought the source of such UFOs might be. If he didn't think they existed, he would have, without a doubt, said so, since nobody likes to have the stigma of being "a UFO nut" attached to their careers.

Such a label never helps in that regard. So not to deny the existence of them, and even to go further, to say where he thought they were from, says a lot. It says he may actually have witnessed some UFOs during his flight, but if so, he's not going so far as to say that.

And who can blame him if this is so. Many commercial pilots have had their flying careers ruined for daring to report sightings of UFOs. And with NASA's silence on the subject, it doesn't seem likely they would be happy with any of their astronauts making such statements, either.

Yet, despite this veil of silence NASA has consistently imposed on the subject of UFOs, their refusal to comment on the topic at virtually all times, it's then surprising to us just how many astronauts have come forward to speak about it. Of course, some of their broadcasts were public, so in some instances, denial would have been rather pointless on their part, when everyone has access to those particular transcripts in such cases.

Apollo 11 Astronauts Neil Armstrong and Edwin Aldrin. Now, of course, we come to that perhaps most famous astronaut of all, Neil Armstrong. His contribution to the question of the existence of aliens and aliens on the Moon is of a more controversial nature.

Publicly, he said nothing on the subject. However, according to Dr. Vladimir Azhazha, Astronaut Neil Armstrong told his superiors on Earth there were two objects watching them near where they had landed on the Moon. He said the objects were large and were situated not far from the landing module. This was never made public according to Azhazha.

And another individual, a Dr. Aleksandr Kasantsev, went so far as to say Astronaut "Buzz" Aldrin filmed the UFOs in color, at first from the safety of the interior of the landing module, and later when he and Armstrong exited the vehicle. Again, this film footage, if it exists, was never made public.

However, one source claims that independent verification of UFOs on the Moon during the Apollo landing was made by "ham" (shortwave) radio operators, who, not relying on the rebroadcasts by NASA, listened in to the original transmissions on their own, as they were being sent back from the Moon.

Now the reason why we say this matter with Armstrong is controversial is because Armstrong himself has chosen to keep virtually silent all this time on the subject, and not confirmed any of this. That would certainly make one question the validity of one, or perhaps even both of these professional men (they both have PhDs), but luckily there is one more source which claims that all this, in fact, happened, and it's a reliable source.

Maurice Chatelain. Mr. Chatelain was at one time the chief of NASA Communications. This means he is a man of no little repute, and one who undoubtedly carried security clearances, as well. In other words, his reputation and qualifications are solid.

Mr. Chatelain publicly has declared that Neil Armstrong did see and report UFOs being on the Moon. He further claims the incident was known throughout the confines of NASA, but was never publicly spoken of.

The former chief goes further. He says all the flights of both the Gemini and Apollo programs were followed, watched, with the UFOs sometimes coming incredibly close to the human vessels, perhaps dangerously so. He said all the astronauts religiously reported such events, and were then invariably ordered to be silent about it.

Mr. Chatelain further states he believes the astronauts coined the code term "Santa Claus," to inform Mission Control of when they spotted UFOs (seen "Santa Claus"). Mr. Chatelain even suggests that when Astronaut James Lovell, in 1968, and while onboard the Apollo 8 Command module as it completed its orbit of the far side of the Moon on Christmas Day, said, *"Please be informed there is a Santa Claus."*

Was this just a joke because it was Christmas? It could well have been. No one knows for sure, except the people involved. But the term, "Santa Claus," has been used by other astronauts, as well, and it was nowhere near Christmastime when they did. So we leave it to you to decide this matter.

There is more of this sort of thing, as well, but the truth is if all these testimonies and comments by various (eleven cited here) astronauts and pilots aren't enough to convince someone they saw UFOs, think they exist, and/or think they are from "elsewhere" and so extraterrestrial, than citing more such examples won't help.

Please do remember; these men were all picked because they supposedly had the "right stuff." However, in the final analysis, it must be up to you, the reader, to choose to believe what they have to say on the subject of aliens in our skies. Only you can decide if these astronauts really had the "right stuff" in your personal opinion, the "stuff" necessary for you to believe what they have said on the subject of UFOs, if it is true.

Chapter Conclusion. Our purpose in listing these astronauts and others, and their main comments on this subject was to add to the overall body of evidence to support the idea the Moon is a focus of attention by aliens. To recap, we have already shown the Moon has a lot of strange anomalies about it. We've also illustrated that none of the current theories of the origins completely explain all this, and so new theories, as recently as 2011, are still being promulgated to attempt to do this, while older ones are being constantly modified (and therefore made increasingly complicated and unlikely) to attempt to solve these issues.

We've also discussed two noted Russian scientists who originally proposed the Hollow Moon Theory (Spaceship Moon Theory) as another possible origin. We went on to point out that as unlikely as such a theory seems to be, it does account for all the oddities about our Moon, if true.

Of course, for the idea to have validity there must be actual aliens in space and on the Moon who might have accomplished such a colossal feat. And that is why we've included this last chapter about astronauts and their views on the subject of aliens and UFOs, to further validate the fact that aliens exist, and have been seen on the Moon. The chapter on photographs taken of the Moon and "structures" there also helps to act as corroboration.

Now, having added to the support for the Hollow Moon Theory in this way, with these additional "legs," we'll next look at some more current information and possible evidence for the idea. This will include testimony by those who weren't astronauts, but were contractors for NASA. They insist the agency is covering up evidence for the existence of aliens on our lunar neighbor. We will also delve into and discuss some evidence for strange events still occurring on the Moon.

CHAPTER 11

NASA COVERUP—"A Shadowy Government?"

"There exists a shadowy Government with its own Air Force, its own Navy, its own fundraising mechanism, and the ability to pursue its own ideas of the national interest, free from all checks and balances, and free from the law itself."

—Senator Daniel K. Inouye

Now in our discussions about the likelihood of aliens on the Moon and the hollow Moon idea, we have to turn to yet some more possible evidence. This is yet another leg on which to stand our Hollow Moon Theory. This evidence although not directly from NASA itself, is said to be attributable to that organization from those who had either once worked for NASA, or worked as subcontractors for companies that did business directly for NASA, and so they were onsite at its various locations. This much about them is not a matter of controversy or contention. They have been checked and their statements in this respect are known to be true.

However, the following evidence is contentious. It presumes, if one believes the people who relate the information, that NASA is actively involved in a cover-up of the idea of their being aliens on or in the Moon. This is a weighty charge, indeed. So it should be considered with great care. After all, I'm no more inclined to ruin the reputation of an organization, private or governmental, without good cause, any more than I'd care to wantonly sabotage the reputation of any individual.

So just why is this evidence so contentious? Well, because it strongly suggests NASA, a nominally civilian agency, must be taking directions from someone else, someone who has the power to order them to commit such cover-ups, such outright fraud, if you will. Since NASA is also a government agency, as well, then the only possible "humans" with such power must be the military and/or perhaps them in tandem with some secretive governmental agency.

Whether this secretive agency is the C.I.A, some military cabal, or whatever, the results are still the same if this is true. That is, a virtual shadow government is controlling the outflow of any information regarding aliens here and on the Moon.

Does the idea of a shadow government seem preposterous to you? Does it evoke images of paranoia, conspiracy-theorist "nuts?" Of course, it probably would. However, before we react too negatively to the idea of such a hidden group or agency doing such a thing as hiding information regarding aliens, let's just check out a few facts, first.

Here's a quotation from an American President, one who was highly revered for having directed the European Theatre of World War II for the Allies, meaning of course, President Dwight D. Eisenhower. In 1961, he publicly stated:

"In the councils of Government, we must guard against the acquisition of unwarranted influence, whether sought or unsought, by the Military Industrial Complex. The potential for the disastrous rise of misplaced power exists, and will persist. We must never let the weight of this combination endanger our liberties or democratic processes. We should take nothing for granted. Only an alert and knowledgeable citizenry can compel the proper meshing of the huge industrial and military machinery of defense with our peaceful methods and goals so that security and liberty may prosper together."

To this day, anyone who speaks of the often (seemingly) too-close relationship between our military and our industry, always tends to use the term "Military-Industrial Complex." The warning President Eisenhower invokes in this statement is blatant, bold, and meant to be taken very seriously. In short, he must have had real fear of the Military-Industrial Complex in this country to verbalize such a strident and outright warning about it. And remember, for him to have such fears, as the supposedly most powerful person in the world at the time, is saying something.

Therefore, before we shout "Paranoia!" and refer to "conspiracy-theory nuts," maybe we should just stop and consider why he, a President of the United States, felt it necessary to go so far as publicly to warn Americans in such a way. Just why did the President feel compelled to so publicly proclaim the dangers of such a concentrated form of political and military power in the hands of so few, ones not greatly held in check by our normal machinery of government, but rather the reverse?

Moreover, why did Senator Daniel K. Inouye later feel so compelled to say, as shown in the above quotation at the start of this chapter, speak of a "shadowy government," with its own military, air force, and navy, one, as he put it, "free from all checks and balances, free from the law itself?"

Remember, these were highly respected and very powerful men, had long and successful careers in public office. They were not "fly-by-night," fringe-element politicos in the slightest way. So if they say something is so, perhaps, it would more than behoove us to listen to them and maybe consider that what they is so?

If this is the case, if they are sounding the alarm about a shadow government controlling things in our country, with the force of "a military" behind them (presumably, at least a portion of ours), then it is quite reasonable to assume they may be interfering with NASA.

"They" may be controlling what NASA releases in the way of photos and videos of the lunar surface. Either this is true, that such hidden power does exist with such a potential to do such things, or two highly revered former members of our government, one a senator and the other a famous president, were "crazy," which seems highly unlikely, in the extreme.

So if NASA was altering photographs under the orders of such a hidden "shadowy government," how would we ever become aware of such a thing happening? Well, there are only three possible ways, really:

1. NASA itself might decide to make what it has been doing public, regardless of the consequences (which it hasn't),

2. Whistle-blowers might reveal what's going on and show examples, or

3. The secret may come out by an accident or series of accidents.

Since we can rule out NASA publicly proclaiming it has been involved in a major fraud being perpetrated on the American people, than alternatives (2) or (3) are the most likely ways such a thing could be revealed to us. That is, of course, unless there is a combination of alternatives going on, with some members of NASA accidentally revealing what's really happening, as well as some whistle-blowers being involved who are doing the same.

Maybe the accidental release of certain photographs was no accident, but done quite on purpose. Or maybe, the whistleblowers' access to such things wasn't quite so much a case of serendipity, but more of a "set-up" to allow them to discover certain information and then disseminate it to us. There may be factions within NASA who feel different ways about the matter.

Who knows? We may never know what the truth about all this, but one thing is certain, and that is some people, those who were "in the know" claim certain things. We will discuss those people and "things" now.

Donna Hare. Donna is a woman of remarkable capabilities. She worked on a subcontracting basis for NASA for more than fifteen years. And when we say remarkable, we mean remarkable! She has repeatedly won awards for her work.

Among her many talents is that of being a technical artist. Moreover, MS Hare has spent most of her career working in various capacities in the space industry. Her work includes involvement with flight manuals and dealing with various sorts of pictures and illustrations.

During a radio interview in Washington DC, MS Hare claimed that while working for NASA during the time of the Apollo missions, she was made aware of a number of remarkable things. For the sake of brevity and lack of space here in this book, we'll just summarize the main points of the interview here:

1. MS Hare stated she has a security clearance. This has since been verified. It was her understanding, or perhaps misunderstanding, that this clearance gave her authorization to go anywhere on the premises of certain buildings. She entered into a restricted section. There, satellite pictures were developed, including photographs from the Apollo missions. She chatted to one of the technicians. While they talked, he was constructing a mosaic from a number of satellite photos, forming them into one bigger one. NASA does this often.

While gazing at one of the pictures of the mosaic, MS Hare noticed a "dot." When asked about this, the technician told her it was not a flaw in the film, because it was casting a shadow. She could make out some details, for instance, that there were pine trees. The shadow of the "dot" fell upon some of those trees, and when she inquired about this, the technician said he couldn't tell her what it was, since that was forbidden. However, she said he made it clear he meant for her to understand it was a UFO.

When she asked him what his intentions were with regard to the photograph, his response was he would have to airbrush the object out of the picture, that this was his job. No photos were to be released to the public that contained such images of objects.

2. Another thing MS Hare talked about was her discussion with another person, a man she had seen on a personal basis for a while. Part of his task at NASA was to be with the astronauts while they were in quarantine. He told her that while with them, he had learned a great deal.

According to him, all the lunar astronauts had witnessed UFOs. Furthermore, they informed him they had been ordered to be silent on the subject, at the risk of breaching national security, with the penalties of prison sentences, and loss of their pensions and benefits if they were to divulge any of the information.

He also warned MS Hare that if she ever divulged what he said and attributed it directly to him, he would be forced to deny all of what he'd told her. Still, Ms. Hare was convinced he was telling her the truth, at least, as he knew it.

3. Ms. Hare went on to state that with regard to the ill-fated Apollo 13 mission, that she has been told the mission couldn't possibly have made it back to Earth without help and by this, she definitely did not mean help from anyone on Earth.

4. After MS Hare changed jobs, a former guard for NASA entered her office one day. He said it had been his job to burn all the original UFO pictures. Apparently, he wasn't supposed to look at the photographs, because when he lingered over one too long, a member of the military struck him in the head with the butt of his rifle, causing unconsciousness. It would seem this was the origin of a large scar on his forehead according to him. The photo he had been looking at was of an alien ship that had" little bumps" all over it, and looked as if it had been partially burned, or charred. It was down amidst a field of cattle.

5. MS Hare went on to describe that also according to what she'd been told, alien spacecraft trailed all the Apollo trips to the Moon, and were on the Moon, as well. With regard to the disastrous Apollo 13 mission, she said that although the aliens had helped return the vessel to Earth, it might have been them who had interfered with it in the first place, because it was headed to a region of the Moon that was off-limits to humans. She was told there was something there the aliens didn't want us to see or know about, or possibly to interfere with in any way.

Now, the question naturally arises if MS Hare is to be believed? Based on her background, her solid reputation, the links of her career with NASA, and the fact that nothing negative has ever been said or reported about her, one can only assume she is telling the truth, at least as she sees it.

Some of it is hearsay, of course. Some of it is not, as with her seeing the photograph of the saucer hovering over the pine trees. Therefore, it is reasonable to conclude MS Donna Hare is telling us the truth.

Sergeant Karl Wolfe. Sergeant Wolfe is yet another person with a pristine work record, and an unimpeachable background in his career. Sergeant Wolfe worked for the Director of Intelligence at Headquarters Tactical Air Command. This was at Langley Field, Virginia. It is important to note Langley Field was a location that received incoming data from the Orbiter Satellite.

This data was later transferred to actual images. This is done at an NSA-controlled lab. Sergeant Wolfe was one of two lab technicians there. This meant he had a high security clearance to perform his work. This tells us he was trusted, had been vetted. So one has to think if his reputation and credentials were good enough to satisfy the NSA, they should be good enough to satisfy us as to his veracity in these matters.

In any case, one day he was called out to another location on the base. There was a problem with some equipment used for printing images from the Lunar Orbiter program. One should note here the location in question was also under the control of the NSA (the National Security Agency). Sergeant Wolfe said that at the time he was not aware of what the NSA even was. Also note his security status had to be increased in order to allow him access to this location.

Upon arriving there, he was surprised to find how many people there were from other countries, what a strong international presence there was at a place, one he'd assumed was reserved strictly for Americans with security clearances, it being an

American program that required such clearances even to be there, supposedly.

Going on about his business, he entered the lab room holding the equipment requiring repairs. He determined the job was too difficult to do on-site. He arranged to have the equipment transferred.

While Sergeant Wolfe waited for this to happen, he struck up a conversation with an airman on duty. Curious, he inquired why the film development and printing was being done at Langley, instead of at a NASA center. The airman told him the pictures first had to be processed, enhanced, and then scrutinized by the military before being released to the general public.

The airman further elaborated. He explained to Sergeant Wolfe there were unidentified edifices clearly to be seen on the far side of the Moon. These were obviously artificial in nature. In short, it appeared there was some sort of a complex or base on the far side of the Moon, one apparently not made by humans.

The news floored Sergeant Wolfe, all the more so when he began to realize the full implications of what he'd heard. When shown the actual photographs, the Sergeant saw exactly what the airman had described, a complex of various structures, including what appeared to be very standard-looking radar dishes, such as we have here on our world.

Now the sergeant realized why so many international personnel were present at the facility. Obviously, they were there because of the things in the photographs. Of course, even at the time, it was obvious to the sergeant that these were not photos of bases built by Americans, Russians, or anyone else on Earth. The technology and the means were simply not yet available to do such a thing. The base had to have been constructed by "someone else."

Sergeant Wolfe was made to understand that all such images were being carefully removed from the photographs, airbrushed out, the pictures changed so such things would no longer appear in them. The public, it seemed, was not to be allowed to know about any of this, anything to do with the idea of there being an alien base on the far side of the Moon.

Given the atmosphere of those days, the intensity of the Cold War, Sergeant Wolfe understood this. The implications and ramifications of releasing such material might even provoke a hot war, if the Russians, for example, thought Americans had access to something, some technology that they did not. Under such circumstances, a preemptive nuclear strike by the Russians to stop us from gaining too much of an advance over them in technology certainly wouldn't have been out of the question.

So at the time and for this reason, because of fear of reprisals, and even the possibility of a prison term, or worse, Sergeant Wolfe remained silent about what he had seen and heard that day. Even after he left the military, because of the terms of his security clearance, he continued to remain silent. It wasn't until thirty years after the event he finally dared to talk about it.

The Canadian Publication. This publication stated that:

"Dr. Micheal Salla has indicated that there is a Military Industrial Extraterrestrial Complex or MIEC, and that Earth is being assimilated by an alien agenda, which also operates on Earth's Moon."

If this is true, then it would appear humans aren't the only ones with a Military-Industrial Complex. It would seem aliens might have one, as well. If so, is their group and our "shadowy government" group working hand in hand? Worse, could they be one and the same? It would seem distinctly possible.

Clementine Satellite. The Clementine Satellite, launched in 1994, took photographs of the far side of the Moon, among other images of that world. The total number of pictures taken is purportedly to have been almost two million (1.8 million). However, only 170,000 such pictures were ever released. The remainder, which form the vast majority of them, are classified.

Why? Why would literally almost one and a half million photos, many of the far side of the Moon, have to be classified, and then remain so permanently? Again, the only reason for making such images classified is because there must be something about them (in them?) that the U.S. Navy doesn't want the general public to see or know about.

But what could be so unusual about mere photographs of the lunar surface, when supposedly we've seen the entire surface in other photographs since then? It does make one wonder… a lot! We reiterate, why would photographs of mere mountains and craters need to be classified, especially those of the far side of the Moon?

We leave it to you, the reader, to come up with your own answer to this question, but ours is simply, there is something there they do not want us to see, and that something isn't "natural," but artificial or alien in origin.

There are a couple major conclusions we can reach, at the very least:

1. No less than a President of the United States warned against the power of a "Military-Industrial Complex." He clearly stated he feared the influence such a powerful group might have on the democracy of the United States. More than once, he voiced his concerns over this issue and not only quite publicly, but quite forcibly, as well. He was not alone in this worry.

2. Former Senator Inouye of Hawaii went even further. He declared that a shadow government, or as he put it, "shadowy" government already existed, and it very well could have, and had, its own military, including its own Navy and Air Force.

By that, he meant they had the power to direct some of our existing forces to their own ends, and without any due oversight by any congressional or other sitting body to determine if what they did was lawful or correct. They were and are a law unto themselves, answerable to nobody but themselves.

3. We have evidence of photographs of the Moon showing objects on it that by all rights shouldn't even be there. These photos seem to show structures in ruins, as well as perhaps operating structures. These do not appear to be of any Earthly origin.

What's more, when one looks at some of the photos, it does appear as if attempts are made to airbrush out some of the features. However, what worked well back in the early to mid-'60s, doesn't work so well anymore, not with the Photoshop programs people have today, the ability to scan and enlarge pictures now in the hands of just about any person who wishes to have such an ability.

4. We have evidence of literally over a million photographs of the Moon, many of the far side, being classified and then remaining so for decades, and even now, to this very day.

5. We have the testimony of two very reliable witnesses as to seeing and hearing of alien bases on the Moon. Normally, as authors, we don't rely terribly much on the testimony of only one or two witnesses, but there are others, as well.

We didn't include them here simply for the sake of brevity, and because these two persons so included, have such impeccable qualifications, such a history of reliability as witnesses. Again, if security clearances were awarded them by NASA and the NSA, no less, why shouldn't we think them trustworthy? Those organizations certainly did.

There simply is no reason to doubt their word. Furthermore, there is no reason to think they might have misinterpreted what they saw. This is so because of what was also related to them, the fact they saw some of the pictures for themselves, and what they knew from other NASA sources.

One must either believe them or not. There is no middle ground. We choose to believe them, because we think it is more likely what they say is true, than not. They have simply no reason to lie, have lifetime reputations to maintain, ones they would not likely casually throw aside, and because the same reputations show they were highly qualified people doing work in high-security areas of NASA and the NSA.

Our conclusion is there is some type of ongoing, systematic, and well-organized cover-up by NASA, the NSA, portions of the military, and other governmental organizations. Together, these all might form that "shadowy government" spoken of by the Hawaiian Senator.

The evidence would seem to be in, as it were, in this regard. Either that, or a lot of well-credentialed people are lying, and these are people who have no reason to do such a thing. Their entire career history would seem to obviate such a choice as to ruin their credibility, destroy any chance of a future career with NASA, and without having a very good reason to do so.

Yes, they might actually get a book or two out of doing such a thing, but such books do not sell in the millions, and would hardly make up in sales for the cost to them personally in their careers and future incomes. No, these people, at great personal expense to their reputations and positions in society, dared a great deal. We feel for this reason they're telling the truth, because they went to such lengths, to their own personal detriment, and because they are concerned, very concerned, and wanted to tell what they knew about it all.

To further support this contention, let us remind you the photos originally released by NASA in many cases have been removed from their sites, at least, the high-resolution versions that might clearly show something for sure. What are left are only low-resolution photos, and others that seem to clearly have been tampered with. Since these are on NASA's own site, we can't imagine who else would do the tampering, except members of that agency.

Finally, there were those photographs seen in an interview and were quite by chance (or not?) lying on a desk of the interviewee. They clearly show something odd on the Moon. Furthermore, it was in this exact location a satellite then made impact. Either this is a very odd coincidence, or something is actually going on.

Chapter Conclusion. In any case, we feel this is sufficient evidence to create another "leg" on which to base our argument about the idea of aliens being on the Moon, the Moon possibly being hollow, and/or at least having alien bases present there now, and in the past. Combined with the prior evidence we have shown in the other chapters, we think this is an eminently reasonable conclusion.

Are there other conclusions possible? Yes, of course, there are. We do not claim the idea of bases and aliens being on the Moon, and perhaps the Moon being hollow, as an absolute. However, given all the different sources of information we've cited so far, it would appear that this might well be the likely case. We think it more likely, than not.

Combined with the strange attributes of the Moon itself, those transient lunar phenomena which have been witnessed over the centuries, various photographs, comments by astronauts with regard to sighting aliens (many of them), and testimony of witnesses that worked for NASA, this just seems to be probable to us.

Yet there is still more information, which might well be evidence for the idea of the Moon being hollow, and/or aliens having bases there, as well. We'll discuss this information in the next chapter.

CHAPTER 12

Ancient Evidence For A Time Before The Moon?

Was there a time in recorded history when there was no Moon? It would seem a crazy question to ask. Yet, there seems to be a distinct possibility there may have been such a time, because they're actually does seem to be some historical evidence to support the idea.

Moreover, this evidence seems to come from a variety of sources, which would seem to further enforce the idea, to corroborate it. But exactly who is saying this? What are the sources? Well, again, they come from all over. But let's start with something we all should be familiar with, the Bible.

The Bible. The Bible has a number of references to a time when there appears to have been no Moon in the sky. Here are some examples:

Book of Job 22:5 with reference to the time without a moon with the phrase *"before a Moon and it did not shine."*

Psalm 72:5 there is the passage that says: *"Thou wast feared since the sun and before the Moon a generation of generations."*

The Great Flood. According to some legends, it is said the Moon did not appear in the skies above us until after the Great Flood had occurred. This raises the question; did the Moon's arrival create the Great Flood? An initial close pass by the Moon as it settled into orbit around the Earth would have caused massive tides and flooding, not to mention unsettled weather conditions (lots of rain?), as well. Now, let's shift gears and mention the ancient Greeks and Romans with regard to the Moon's "arrival."

Aristotle. Aristotle refers to a period when the Earth was "Moonless." Granted, the references to this are some of the oldest recorded legends of humanity, but then they refer to an event, if it did occur, that happened in prerecorded history. Aristotle referred to Arcadia in Greece.

Specifically, he spoke of a time before the Hellenes occupied the area, and the prior population was of a race of people known as the Pelasgians. Aristotle recorded the information in his works that these people inhabited the region before there was a Moon. For this reason, he referred to them as the Proselenes, which roughly translated means, "those who were there before there was a Moon."

Democritus and Anaxagoras. To add credence to what Aristotle had to write, there is the matter of Democritus and Anaxagoras. Both of these men wrote of a time when the Earth had no Moon in the night sky. They actually taught this to their students as a fact, not a myth or legend.

Apollonius. Here is yet another reference to a time when the Moon was not in our skies. Apollonius of Rhodes actually mentioned, and this is a direct quote:

"...but not all the orbs were yet in the heavens before the Danai and Deukalion races came into existence and only the Arcadians lived of whom it is said that they dwelt on mountains and fed on a course before there was a Moon."

So it would seem there is more than one source for the story of the Arcadians living at a time before the Moon was in our night skies.

Ovid. Judging by the number of comments by various historians, ancient Romans were not to be left out of this idea. Ovid stated that:

"The Arcadians are said to possess their land before the birth of Joseph, and the folk is older than the Moon."

Hippolytus. And here we have yet another reference to the Arcadian people, known here as the Pelasgus. Hippolytus stated that:

"Arcadia brought forth Pelasgus, of greater antiquity than the Moon."

Plutarch. And another famous Roman, Plutarch, commented in The Roman Questions that:

"There were Arcadians of the Evander's following, the so-called pre-Lunar people."

Lucian. In his work, Astrology, Lucian also states that:

"The Arcadians affirm in their folly that they are older than the Moon."

Obviously, Lucian didn't believe them. And yet the references to these people and the fact they existed at a time before there was a Moon reverberated throughout the Pan-Hellenic culture for centuries.

Censorinus. And the very last Roman we intend to mention, Censorinus, also speaks about a time when the night sky was still Moonless.

So it would seem that in the Western world of ancient days, as well as the Middle Eastern region, with record to their written records, oral traditions, legends and all, seem to speak of a time before there was a Moon.

But it isn't just in the Old World in which these odd statements keep appearing, but in traditions of the New World peoples, as well.

Cordilleras of Colombia. An Indian tribe dwelling in this mountain a region of Colombia preface some of their tales of early times, meaning the history of their people, as being before "the Moon inhabited the night sky." For the Chibchas people, they often preface their stories by saying "in the earliest times, when the Moon was not yet in the heavens."

Pictographs, Tiahuanco, Bolivia. In Bolivia, close to the site of those ancient ruins of Tiahuanaco, at the Courtyard of Kalasasaya, pictographs, or hieroglyphs, mention a strange event, that the Moon didn't appear in the night skies until (based on who interprets the dating of those hieroglyphics) around 12,000 years ago, give or take 500 to 1,000 years.

Mayans. The Mayans, as stated in some of their ancient records, said it was Venus that dominated the night sky, that there was no Moon back then to rival the planet.

Now by any standards and at the very least, it must be considered odd that various peoples, totally unrelated geographically and often highly isolated, existing in different areas of the world, separated by an ocean, all seem to have belief systems or records that state the Moon was not always in the sky.

If one goes by these records and the statements of multiple historians from the past, even from such great powers of the time as Rome and Athens were, it would appear the Moon entered orbit around us at about the time civilization began. This was just slightly before written records were being kept.

How very coincidental. The Moon suddenly appears in our skies and humanity also "as if overnight," as some archaeologists put it, develops civilization. Is it really just a coincidence? One does wonder.

It further seems likely that the Moon's arrival may have precipitated, that is, caused the Great Flood, as well. We all know full well the Moon has a strong influence on the Earth in the way of tides, causing them to ebb and flow. And many argue the Moon always had to be here, because records of various civilizations refer to the ebb and flow of tides from the earliest times.

However, the first thing to remember is if the Moon did enter its present orbit just before the start of civilization, it would predate all those written records, so of course tides would be mentioned in them because they were written after the Moon arrived. Secondly, the sun, too, causes tides, and though not as pronounced as the Moon's effects, there would still have been some tides even without the Moon's presence.

Also, if the Moon entered Earth's orbit by first swinging closer to it, before adopting its present and strangely circular orbit, then at its nearest approach, a huge tide or tides would have resulted. Depending on just how close the Moon may have come, the result could have been a catastrophic tide or series of such destructive tides that could well have flooded coastal regions worldwide. It would even have resulted in the flooding of inland areas, as well, especially where they were lowlands, adjacent to river deltas, etc. Is this the origin of the legend, one so many cultures and civilizations around the world have of the Great Flood?

Again, according to the date set by the tribes-people in Bolivia, as well as what information we can gather from the other sources listed here it does appear the Moon may well have come into our skies mere millennia, instead of billions of years ago.

If so, this event would have had a powerful effect on humanity, and in more ways than one. Was the mere arrival of the Moon enough to kick-start civilization? Or, if aliens maneuvered that orb here, did they then arrive on Earth and influence our sudden development? Again, it is odd how civilization began about the same time it is said the Moon arrived in orbit around the Earth. So are the two events totally unrelated? It would be highly questionable to believe so.

It should also be restated here that historians and archaeologists, in general, cannot account for the sudden "explosion" (as many of them put it) of civilization. Instead of a record of a slow climb to the creation of our first cities and the use of metals, etc., all this seems to have happened virtually "overnight," again, as archaeologists tend to describe the event.

Something happened to cause this. The sudden appearance of a satellite in our skies, and the influx of aliens in the form of numerous visitations to Earth may have had something to do with this sudden rise of humanity to civilization. Remember, this was after countless millennia of no apparent development in this regard at all, or at least so little as to be unnoticeable.

So again, did the Moon wander into an orbit around the Earth precisely when human civilization is supposed to have begun by sheer coincidence? If so, it is certainly defying incredible odds to have happened in such a way.

And there are those who believe there are no such things as coincidences. Furthermore, the idea the advent of the Moon into our night skies might have caused the Great Flood is also intriguing, because that is precisely what such an event would cause in all likelihood. You don't shift planets around, large or small, without consequences, and more often than not, serious ones.

In any case, we have corroborative evidence in the form of written and verbal records of these various peoples, claiming there was a time when the Moon did not inhabit our sky. If this is true, then the Moon may have been a very recent arrival on the scene, having entered orbit around Earth perhaps no more than 10,000 to 20,000 years ago.

There is something else to consider here as well. If the Moon actually arrived in orbit around the Earth after humanity was already well established on the planet, then this means the Moon could not have originated based on any of our current scientific theories for its formation, which would have required major cataclysms, even extinction-level ones, to have occurred on Earth in the process.

Somehow, someway, it appears the Moon might just have been captured by the Earth, whether by the influence of "someone's" guiding hand, or by mere chance. This is true, if one is to believe the historical statements/evidence cited above.

Is such evidence enough to prove on its own the idea of a hollow Moon coming to our skies? No, we don't think so, but when one combines it with all the other evidence we've already included here, it does add to a rather convincing argument, a growing body of evidence for this to have possibly occurred. After all, we've cited scientific oddities about the Moon. We've gone into detail about strange "transient lunar phenomena from one of NASA's own lengthy reports.

Furthermore, we've reported what quite a number of astronauts have said regarding aliens, and aliens being on the Moon. Also, we've referenced a number of NASA's own photographs, and related testimony by former NASA employees and contractors with regard to structures and or alien bases on the Moon.

Then, too, we even included the scientific theory by two Russian astronomers, members of the Russian Academy of Science, who made a serious effort to raise the issue of the Moon's origin, and that it may be hollow.

Chapter Conclusion. We feel, at this point, the idea of the Moon being hollow and having arrived on the scene much later than many scientists believe, is at least a very distinct possibility, one with a good deal of corroborative evidence to support it from all these varying sources.

But is there yet even more evidence for the idea of a hollow Moon? Well, if there was another Moon that might be hollow, as well, this would certainly lend more credence to the idea that ours could be hollow, too. In our next chapter, we will consider this possibility.

CHAPTER 13

Corroborating Evidence—Another Hollow Moon?

We've deliberately discussed a number of sources of evidence for our contentions the Moon may be hollow and aliens may now, and have in the past, occupied that sphere. The idea behind this method, as previously mentioned, is simple; the more sources of such information/evidence one can find to substantiate an idea, the more evidentiary "legs" we can provide to make it stand, the more likely the idea is valid. This follows as a matter of course.

It's rather like a wooden stool, to use an old analogy. Three legs are enough to support a stool, but they are the minimum. Such a stool will still rock, be patently unsafe to sit on under certain circumstances. In other words, the stool just isn't reliable enough to trust.

However, the more legs you add to it, the more stable the stool becomes, until it is finally, rock-solid firm and safe to sit on, even safe enough for small children to rest comfortably there, which is no easy thing to achieve.

That's what we're trying to do here, make our proverbial wooden stool, the Hollow Moon Theory and aliens, as firm and stable an idea as possible. If the oddities of our Moon are not enough to convince you, then remember we've provided a great deal of other evidence, such as the fallacies of the origin theories and much more.

Although the mainstream origin theories of the Moon have such "big holes" in them, if this doesn't sway you in your perceptions of the Hollow Moon Theory, then remember all those bona fide reports by so many more-than-competent astronauts about spotting aliens. Were they all lying? Were men we trusted to fly incredibly expensive missions to outer space and to even land on the Moon not to be trusted?

Perhaps, one unreliable or undependable astronaut might slip through the NASA safety net, but so many? Such an idea is incomprehensible to us. The majority of those who say they've seen UFOs and alien vessels must therefore be telling the truth as they saw it.

However, if even these testimonies by our nation's space heroes do not convince you, are insufficient for you to countenance the idea of aliens and/or a hollow Moon, then do think back about those public statements by former, high-echelon, NASA directors, as well as those high-security cleared employees and subcontractor technicians who say much the same thing.

Can all this evidence be irrelevant to you? If so, then let's find yet another source to support the idea the Moon may be hollow and aliens may now or have once resided upon it.

More than one hollow moon? Now, it is logical to consider the idea that if there is one hollow moon in our solar system, there might well be, at least, two. However, if possible, why should such a thing be a logical assumption?

Well the answer is simple. If one can make one hollow moon, why not make more than one? If they serve a specific purpose, then another moon could serve one, as well. In other words, if there is some grand purpose for such hollow moons, having more than one might merely be expedient.

Of course, one must weigh such a thing against the tremendous costs and the incredible effort involved in creating a hollow moon. Even for an advanced technology such as aliens might have, this probably would still be no small effort, almost assuredly. Therefore, you must have some important goal in order to want even to make one hollow moon, let alone two or more.

What use is a hollow moon? So what might be the reason for creating such an elaborate, time-consuming, and expensive thing? What would be the primary function of a hollow moon? Well, one of the uses might be so you could closely observe or interact with planets that might have, or once had life on them. They could be used as massive observation platforms, nearby command centers, bases, and residences for such aliens. In short, they would be a very permanent sort of space station on a grand scale.

So hollow moons just might be ideal as long-term bases, as hubs of operations, places from which such beings could fly to a nearby planet that may have life on it, and easily return. What do they want with a planet that has living things upon it? That, we will discuss later. For now, we wish to concentrate on the idea "they" simply do wish to have such a base near such a type of world. Would this then be a rational reason for a hollow moon to be near a world with life on it?

Yes, this would be a sensible assumption for the use of, or at least one of the possible uses of a hollow moon. Now, taking this assumption, let's do a little easy extrapolation.

If our basic idea is right and hollow moons may be used in conjunction with planets with life on them, then perhaps we can say those planets in our solar system that may have had life once, or have it now, should then have a hollow moon orbiting nearby. This would be a simple next step in the logical process, right?

Moreover, we can go a step further. It would seem since there may well be a large hollow moon near our Earth, that one of the conditions has already been satisfied with regard to our basic assumption, hollow moons orbit planets with life. However, this step is also a little self-serving for us, since it involves some circular logic as it stands.

After all, we have a hollow moon we think is orbiting around our planet, so we say that hollow moons must orbit around planets that have life. And of course, ours does and so we have come full circle in our logic. What we need here is some other planet that might have a hollow moon orbiting around it, as well.

Therefore, here we hit a snag in our deductive reasoning. We need more than one example of this to make our premise hold water, as it were. To resolve the issue, we'd need another planet with life, one close enough to us to be able to know this. Therein lays our problem. We don't know of any other worlds that harbor life on them.

Yes, we have hopes other planets or moons in our solar system, such as Europa, might have life on them, but we have no idea if they really do, or ever did, except, possibly, for one world. Although it may well not have life now, it seems it might likely have had it in the past. This planet, of course, is Mars.

The very latest data from Mars shows it was once a wet world, and had an atmosphere not dissimilar to Earth's when it was young. In addition, a controversial Martian meteorite would appear to contain the fossil remnants of microbes. Again, this is a contentious piece of rock, with scientists lining up on both sides of the argument on this topic, being both for and against the idea.

However, as of now it looks as if it might just actually contain fossils of some sort. No explanations for the structures in the stone, at this point, seem adequately to explain them any other way. So this leaves the idea of the structures being microscopic fossils as still the most likely and viable explanation. That is, unless new findings eventually show otherwise. So far, they haven't. Instead, they tend to corroborate the idea the stone does contain microscopic fossils.

Combined with the latest evidence from Mars from the Rovers exploring that world, their evidence for water having once existed there in abundance, and the corresponding evidence for a once-thicker atmosphere, then it is a reasonable conjecture that life of some sort may once have inhabited Mars. It may have only been microbial in nature, but there is a good chance there was at least that much in the way of life on the red planet and maybe more.

Many scientists even speculate life originated on Earth from Mars, and so in a sense we are all aliens, being Martian in origin, having evolved up from microbes that originated there. Many scientists admit this is conceivably possible, some even say it is likely.

Okay, so we have the fact of there being a good chance for at least one other world in our solar system to have had life on it at some point in the past, if not now. Given our theory that such worlds might, or even should have hollow moons orbiting near them; can we find evidence for this with Mars?

Actually and amazingly, it seems that yes, we most certainly can find such evidence.

A Moon of Mars, Phobos. Mars, as many people may know, has often been referred to as the planet most like Earth, being a "rocky" world, and not one of the bloated gas giants that inhabit our solar system. As mentioned above, it has even been theorized, with some fairly good evidence to support the idea that life once existed on Mars.

Scientists, as also stated above, believe Mars once had water and a much thicker atmosphere. There is even evidence that at one point, the red planet had a magnetic field to protect it from the solar wind, that constant and powerful stream of particles that tries to strip worlds of their atmosphere.

Still there are major differences. Where Earth is around 93 million miles from the sun (approximately), or the equivalent of one Astronomical Unit (AU), Mars is further out, being about 1.52 AU, or a little over half again farther out from the sun than we are. This means its orbit takes longer, almost double that of Earth's year.

And it's a smaller world, considerably. This didn't help it to keep its air, since it had proportionately less gravity to hold it than our planet does. Moreover, it lost its magnetic shield. For millions, perhaps billions of years now, Mars has slowly been losing its atmosphere. What was once a warm wet world is now cold, dry, and deadly to life as we know it, at least on the surface.

There is another major difference. Mars has two moons instead of our one, and they are very small, indeed, compared to our Moon. Their names are Deimos and Phobos, which mean "Horror" (or "Terror" as some translations have it), and "Fear," respectively. They are fitting names for celestial handmaidens to Mars, the God of War. Phobos is the larger of the two Moons by far, and the closest one to Mars.

However, so small are the moons in general, they present certain problems for scientists. In fact, many scientists don't think they are "moons" in the standard sense of the term at all, that they didn't actually form in orbit around the planet Mars. (But then there is also evidence our Moon didn't either.)

Asaph Hall, an American astronomer, discovered both of the "moons" in 1877. However, because they are so small, many think they might have been captured, and are nothing more than satellites of the planet, in the sense that we launch satellites into orbit around the Earth. Many scientists concluded, therefore, the Martian moons might well be nothing more than captured asteroids, since Mars is so close to the Asteroid Belt. This conclusion seemed to content most astronomers for many decades.

However, some people had and still have problems with this idea. Among them, was I. S. Shklovsky, a doctor of astrophysics. After careful research and having repeatedly calculated the orbit of Phobos, he found he had major problems with the moons-as-captured-asteroids theory. For him, things just did not seem to add up, literally.

Before we get deeper into the subject, we have an important side note. It is important to remember that this isn't some "fringe element scientist" we are talking about here. Dr. I. S. Shklovsky is the co-author of the book Intelligent Life in the Universe. He, along with the very famous Cornell professor, Carl Sagan, again, known for the PBS series, Cosmos, together wrote the popular book. So Doctor Shklovsky is a force to be reckoned with in his field.

In any case, again, he had problems with the moon of Mars, Phobos. In particular, he had problems with its orbital motion. For one thing, the moon rolled along in its orbit, or "tumbled." This was unusual for any moon to do. Besides this, Doctor Shklovsky, like many other scientists, also felt certain the moons were just too small.

Compared to any other moons anywhere in our solar system, Deimos and Phobos just didn't fit. They were miniscule by comparison to those other worldlets. In other words, they weren't "normal." Phobos is only about seven miles in radius (fourteen miles in diameter, but it isn't a "round" world, so that's just a rough approximation). Actually, at its longest point, it is almost seventeen miles in length. This still makes for a very small moon, indeed.

As for the idea they originally had been asteroids and had been somehow captured by Mars at some point in its history, well, this didn't seem too likely to Doctor Shklovsky. He reasoned they couldn't be where they were in orbit around the planet, if such an origin was correct. They were in an inappropriate orbital plane for this. Also, both moons are terribly close to Mars. Their orbits around the planet are indeed swift, with Phobos taking less just a little over seven hours to complete its circle about that world.

Also, the moon, Phobos, has a very odd shape. Again, it does not fit the shape any other moons or moonlet in our solar system we presently know of. This shape includes a number of craters, including the largest one, named Stickney, for Astronomer Hall's wife. There seem to be some cracks, or fissures on the moon, as well.

One Soviet spacecraft did notice what would seem to have been gas escaping from the interior. Just what this gas might be is anyone's guess, but some astronomers think it may be water vapor, and that there might be ice at the center of the moon. Maybe, and maybe not; nobody seems to know for sure.

There are some other interesting facts about the moon, Phobos, as well. And this one particular fact was of specific concern to Doctor Shklovsky. And it's one you've heard before here in this book, about another moon, meaning ours.

You see, the density of Phobos is just too low. Yes, you read correctly. Here we have another moon whose density is too low for the size of the object it is. Sound familiar? It should. Our Moon seems to have the same problem.

However, with Phobos, in order for it to be solid and not hollow, that little Moon would have to have the density of less than a standard cloud of water vapor here on Earth. In other words, it would drift through our blues skies like a puffy white cloud.

That of course, isn't the case. Photos show the moon to have features, irregular ones, but features nonetheless. Consequently, it has substance, solid substance. So the only other explanation for this low density is that it is hollow. Shklovsky, after studying his calculations, said a possible explanation could be that Phobos was even composed of a thin layer of metal! Sound familiar, rather like that "metal hull" the Spaceship Theory of our Moon talks about?

But how does one then account for the present photographic appearance of Phobos? Well, there could be a layer of regolith, or loose rock (probably of asteroid origin) lying over the metal. This would be just as there might be with our Moon, according to the Hollow Moon Theory regarding it.

Based on Shklovsky's calculations of the acceleration of that wordlet's orbital motion, he estimated Phobos could well be the equal of a hollow globe of iron. The diameter of this globe would be about ten miles across, but could be no more than two and one-third inches (approximately) in thickness.

Then there was another item that bothered Shklovsky. Phobos seemed to change the speed of its orbit on occasion, which seemed patently impossible on the face of it, at least, not without something truly extraordinary going on. This is a controversial topic, with some scientists saying it is merely due to discrepancies in the calculations. Again, maybe, and maybe not.

Do recent photos of Phobos show a "natural-looking world?" Yes, they do. And recent calculations of the density are consistent with the idea that Phobos may be a "rubble pile," as one astronomer put it. However, even so, there would still have to be "voids" (empty spaces or caverns, or something of that order) for even the best and most recent calculation of that moon's density to be valid. In other words, no matter how one approaches the matter, it would seem Phobos is either hollow or has large hollows within it.

In other words, it fits the Hollow Moon Theory pattern very nicely.

Besides this, there is the orbit of Phobos. Scientists simply can't account for it. It was Shklovsky's theory that only an artificially entered into orbit could explain the weirdness of Phobos' so-close, so-speedy, and so strange orbit around Mars. In his opinion, nothing else adequately accounted for such an atypical orbit. He believed that Phobos might actually be, in fact, a huge spacecraft, if albeit, a camouflaged one. Again, this rings familiar bells, because our Moon has a highly unusual orbit, as well.

One final thing, Phobos has a "monolith" on it, a large, three-sided object that sticks up quite high. Scientists theorize (and it is only a theory) that it is the remnant of another object striking Phobos. Still, when one considers the "Tower" on the Moon, and the so-called "pyramid" on Mars, it is a tantalizing object about which one would like to know more. There is even a possible, unmanned, robotic trip talked about being sent to Phobos to land near the monolith, so curious are scientists about it.

Chapter Conclusion. Does all this sound very familiar to you? It should. And isn't this exactly what the Hollow Moon Theory claims could be true of our own Moon? So there may be not just one, but actually two hollow moons/spaceships in our solar system. The fact that each of them revolves around a world that either has or may have had life in the past would then be no mere coincidence. It would be no accident, but done deliberately so. We stress the word "deliberately" here.

And if this is so, then we have yet another new leg to the analogy of our stool, upon which to stand the idea of a hollow moon, and yet more evidence that our Moon may, indeed, be hollow, because it could well be that it is not the only one in our solar system.

CHAPTER 14

The Implications Of A Hollow Moon

Of course, a hollow Moon has many implications. And modifying all of these is the main question, the extent to just how large the hollow of the Moon might be? The size of the cavity intensifies any implications, makes them less or more extreme in all probability.

Why is this? Well after all, big packages can hide more than small packages. We're not trying to be facetious here by saying this. If the Moon is hollow and artificially made so, then no one is going to go to the effort, expense, and the time required in creating a vast internal space versus a small one there, if they don't intend to use that extra space for something.

A large space means the purpose was highly important to them in order to justify going to such great lengths to create such a thing. In other words, logic dictates the payoff would have to be worthy of such tremendous expenditure and effort to hollow out something as large as our Moon.

That's not to say a smaller hollow, or series of them, as in caverns, wouldn't have incredible ramifications and implications, as well. We are just talking about a matter of degree here, not whether such a thing would be serious for us or not, because it would, whether a succession of caverns or one colossal cavern.

However, at this point, we move perilously close to the realm of sheer conjecture because of the unavailability of information regarding such a purpose. Still, instead of flights of pure fantasy, can we use the available evidence we do have to try to come to some reasonable conclusions? In other words, is it possible to ascertain from the existing clues just what may actually be going on inside the Moon?

The answer to this is a qualified yes. We may not be able to get exact answers to our questions, but we should be able to arrive at reasonably close solutions. So let's take a brief look at what we now think we may know so far, the facts.

Fact: there seems to be a more than reasonable amount of evidence to support the idea and contention that the Moon may be hollow. We base this on the theory of the two Russian scientists. We also base it on the numerous "oddities" about the Moon, testimony of various astronauts regarding aliens in space and on the Moon.

Furthermore, we also base this on historical reports about a "time" before the Moon, as well as the many "transient lunar phenomena," which name we find something of a misnomer, since these "transient" phenomena" have gone on for centuries, and seem to repeat constantly. Of course, we've referred to much more than this here, but this recap will suffice for our purposes as a general basis to support our hollow Moon contention.

Fact: this must have been done (the creation of a hollow Moon) at the very least, many millennia ago, perhaps millions, or even a billion or more years ago. The amount of time is, necessarily uncertain due to the minimal amount of recorded history regarding this subject.

However, we do find some intriguing historical support for this assumption based on several cultures' ancient records. These records support the idea our Moon has been in the sky for at least 11,000 years, but again, perhaps much longer. Moreover, we base this on not just one recorded source, but on historical references made throughout recorded history and from various civilizations around the world.

Fact: again referring to the testimony of astronauts and people who either worked directly for NASA, or were subcontracted to NASA, we see much available evidence for the idea that aliens are on the Moon and/or in and around it.

Photographs of the Moon also would seem to indicate this. Judging by the so-called "ruins," it would seem "they" have been there a very long time. Perhaps the most damning evidence of all in this regard is the attempts by someone or some group to hide and cover up such evidence, a "shadowy government." And there do seem to have been such attempts, if reputable people involved in this are to be believed.

If the Moon is, indeed, hollow as we suspect, then it was done a long time ago, millennia at least, and by aliens, since we have not had and still don't have, the capabilities of accomplishing such a feat. Evidence would strongly suggest the orb has been moved into orbit around Earth on purpose, and for some specific reason or reasons.

The strangeness of the incredibly circular orbit of the Moon and the unlikelihood of this happening naturally, again those numerous trans-lunar phenomena over the centuries, the strange circumstances of the satellite itself, with regard to thickness of crust on the far side, and makeup of surface lunar material, among many other things, would all seem to testify to this fact.

In other words, the Moon is hollow and aliens have made it so. They occupy it now, which we think likely, or they have at least occupied it in the past.

Chapter Conclusion. So there seems to be much evidence for a Hollow Moon in our skies. Now the implication of this, is that it gives rise to a singular question; just why would aliens go through so much trouble? Why would they want a hollow Moon orbiting Earth and possibly Mars? Well, as we mentioned earlier, the answer might well be life is involved somehow, or has been in the past, on both these worlds.

Still, our next question has to be, what hides in a hollow moon? This, we will discuss in the next chapter.

CHAPTER 15

What's In A Hollow Moon?

Now the normal enough question, one that must inevitably arise, is just what exactly would be inside a hollow Moon? Why bother to hollow one out, even to create one? Well, let's take a closer look at all this, and perhaps find some reasons why this may be so.

Just why would an alien race want to hollow out a moon? Well, as fantastic as the idea seems, we (meaning us humans) have come up with, and quite independently of the Hollow Moon Theory, the concept of hollowing out asteroids. So this idea isn't nearly as "alien" as one might think.

In fact, on the Internet, one can find a number of cogent proposals for this and ones by very reputable authorities, with well thought out ideas of how exactly to undertake the engineering of such a thing. Why would we want to live inside an asteroid rather than, say, on the surface of a neighboring world such as the Moon or Mars? Well, for one thing, it would be far less expensive to do, in fact could even be profitable, as well as being a far safer habitat for the occupants.

And here's the crux of the matter: if we want to move it to someplace else, this we can accomplish relatively easily. Asteroids can be moved, so we could be a mobile people, able to shift our location. However, what we can't do and won't be able to do for the foreseeable future is travel faster than the speed of light. What do these two things have in common? Why do we mention them together?

Well, if we want to go to even the nearest star, it could take thousands of years. At the speed of the Voyager probe, for instance, it's estimated it would take about 80,000 years! Just to get out past the Ort Cloud, that outer sphere or comet shell would take 30,000 years, and that's only about a light year out from Earth.

We simply don't have the capabilities of getting there quickly. So what's our alternative? We could send people there by ship and somehow put them in suspended hibernation. The only problem with this is we don't know how to do that yet, or if it is possible to do it for so long a time. So it would seem we are back to the proverbial "square one."

The only other alternative is to build a generational ship. No matter how one looks at it, this is an expensive and problematic proposition at best. The ship would have to be huge. The vessel would have to be completely self-contained with everything recycled, at least for long enough to get the ship to the nearest star system where it might be able to refuel and resupply itself. The passengers would have to live and die on board the ship. Each generation would have to take up where the last left off. They would have to do this for about 80,000 years or perhaps much, much longer if we wished to travel farther. Could we even build a ship to last that long?

This, in itself, is also problematic. Societies change over time. Children don't want to do what their parents originally wanted them to do. Goals and objectives change with each generation.

For instance, the concept of what we consider America to be today is far different than what the founding fathers originally envisioned. Our country today is a product of each generation modifying those original terms and conditions of our country and its society. The same would hold true on board the generational ship. And again, to build one in space, which is the only way we could manage it, would be hideously expensive, time-consuming, and involve enormous feats of engineering.

Could we do it? Yes, we probably could. It would take decades to accomplish, though, and would probably require the efforts of multiple nations, if not the entire world to achieve, as well as every last bit of cutting-edge technology we could employ in the process. So to build such a ship from scratch would be, again, rather problematic.

Luckily, we have an alternative to this idea of a generational ship. This would be using asteroids. We could use either one or more. The advantage of this would be that we could live inside the asteroid, hollow it out. Propulsion systems could be loaded into it, even atomic ones. People could actually live in the asteroid while it was being modified. This means they wouldn't have to worry about solar flares, and resulting radiation storms.

Moreover, this would also mean we would not have to try to ship everything up from Earth orbit, and build it from scratch. This would mean billions in savings. Some asteroids are made entirely of metals, such as nickel and iron. This means it would be far cheaper for us to put a small foundry on the asteroid to convert this metal into structural implements for the asteroid ship, rather than to have to try to lift all the material out of the huge gravity well that is Earth.

If an asteroid was moved to near Earth orbit, other metals of it could be sent back to Earth. Many asteroids are rich in such metals as Iridium, Gold, Silver, Platinum, Rubidium, as well as many other less precious, but still necessary metals, such as Zinc, Aluminum, Iron, etc. This would certainly help compensate for the cost of such a major construction project.

For instance, one asteroid alone could be worth a fortune. Why? Well one estimate says that a single such asteroid would be worth **NINE TRILLION DOLLARS!** That's more than the entire world's gross national product for a year!

There are many other advantages, as well. Such an asteroid ship could hold an enormous number of people, a veritable city or small country, and be self-supporting. Furthermore, it could be made to rotate to give Earth-level gravity for the inhabitants in the form of centrifugal force. An asteroid would provide much more protection with its thick exterior of stone or solid metal (relative to the very thin skin of the ship) against meteors, radiation, and such.

Would it also be difficult to achieve? Yes, it would and it would take a considerable amount of time. But again, if an asteroid was moved to near Earth orbit, the metals of it could be sent back to Earth and this would compensate for the cost of such a major construction project. And remember, this method would also save thousands of very expensive, space-suited man and woman hours of spacewalks building the superstructure of a giant habitat/ship from scratch, and lifting all those components up from Earth.

Now back to that question of what we would do with such a habitat. Besides creating large, self-sustaining, off-world population centers in case something were to happen to our planet, and thus ensuring the survival of the human species, we will also in the process have created habitats that are more comfortable and safer than living on the surface of any world.

Think about the dangers of living on the surface of the Earth, for example. We have bad weather in the form of hurricanes, tornadoes, flooding rain storms, blizzards, droughts, and more. We have volcanoes. We have tsunamis. We have earthquakes. Then of course, there is the risk of a major solar flare, or even a cosmic ray burst.

In short, living on the surface of the world, any world for that matter is a rather risky proposition. However, living inside an asteroid, with its thick walls of metal and/or stone, we would be much safer. Would there be some risks? Of course, there always are in this reality we exist in. However, they would be far less in number and degree in many cases than living outside, in the open, on a planet's surface, including even the surface of our Earth.

What's more, it would obviate, make totally unnecessary, the idea of colonizing the surface of other planets. Why bother? Why not just live in space permanently, where there is an abundance of solar energy, and materials?

For instance, the Asteroid Belt is vast. It would take hundreds of thousands of years or perhaps much longer to use up the resources in it. And how about all those necessary volatiles we'd need? Here, we're referring to such things as oxygen, nitrogen, hydrogen, water, carbon and other necessary ingredients. We need those to support life.

Well, most scientists are sure there is a vast amount of that "out there." A great deal of it resides in the form of comets and plutons (Pluto-like worldlets) in the Kuiper Belt and with comets in the Oort Cloud.

Estimates are there could be trillions of comets out there, great big balls of dirty ice. Ice is water, and so is made up of hydrogen and oxygen. So we would have plenty of water, as well as air. And many asteroids have a lot of carbonaceous material in them, as well as ones being all of different metals. So getting what we need to survive would be no problem, again, if we are willing to travel "out there." This means our asteroid habitats would ultimately decide to reside further out from the sun, away from the dangers of our star, its attendant radiation and risk of solar flares, and thus farther out than our Planet Earth is.

Moreover, we already know there are star systems that have debris belts around them, stars in early formation of their own systems, with planets not yet fully formed. This means that in all likelihood, asteroid belts, Oort clouds, and Kuiper belts are common things in our galaxy. Other stars would seem to have them, too. So there is a strong incentive, an allure, and urge to travel farther and farther away from our sun.

What would we use for energy? Well, we have atomic power at our disposal in the form of fission, and perhaps in the near future, fusion, as well. These could not only supply energy for the asteroid habitats, but power propulsion systems, too.

In short, we have everything we need. Moreover, we have just illustrated there would be a natural tendency for us to migrate farther and farther away from the center of our solar system. We'd travel out to its extreme edges. Besides this, we've also shown that many other solar systems would be similar to ours, in the respect of having the necessary materials to create even more such habitats.

What exactly are we saying here? Well, we're saying the future of the human race may be a diaspora to the stars. And it may not need to find new planets to live on, or have the necessity of using "spaceships" as we think of them. Instead, we would convert asteroids to our purposes.

Why would we go? To explore, yes, we would definitely do that. To try to find other life and other intelligence would be high on our agenda, no doubt, as well. To expand the sum total of human knowledge would definitely be another criterion.

But it is doubtful that many would actually choose to travel to other stars to try to live on another planet, to try to acclimate to an alien ecology (assuming there even was one) and unknown conditions on worlds that could be exceedingly dangerous for humans. Remember, after living generations inside an asteroid, having everything you need, as well as safety and security, that then has become their home.

For example, a planet that may already sustain life, life that might be compatible with ours, and have an oxygen atmosphere and water, could still be a death sentence for us. All it would have to have it is a little too much beryllium dust in its atmosphere, as just one instance. Beryllium dust is a poison to us. We can only tolerate very small amounts of it. So such a planet might look like paradise, but would be unfit for human habitation. Again, the easy answer is just to reside inside of hollowed-out asteroids or moonlets. There, we completely control the environment. We know it's safe, because we would have made it so.

Finally, when talking about asteroids and the hollowing out of them to create habitats for us, there is one terribly important thing to remember: this is not some fantastical, pie-in-the-sky scheme. We have the capability of doing all this right now. We have, with our current technological abilities, the necessary competence actually to do this today. We don't need some future forms of technology not yet invented.

Yes, again, it would be very expensive to do the first one. However, once it was completed, it could be used as an in-space base to create more. In other words, the first hollowed-out asteroid would become the factory and base of operations for making many more and much more cheaply, because you wouldn't have to ferry all the equipment and personnel up from Earth each time. They could live on board the already hollowed-out asteroid and mass produce what is needed on location.

Carl Sagan was quoted as having said:

"Conceivably, the capture and hollowing of a small asteroid may be technically more feasible than the construction in orbit of an artificial satellite with material brought from the surface."

So there we have it. One of the most famous cosmologists even thinks it's a preferable idea to building a space station from scratch, and far cheaper, too.

Why are we going on at such length about howling-out asteroids? Well, let's think about that. Today, if we have, with our existing technological capabilities the resources of doing this, then why shouldn't other intelligences have the same capabilities?

Intelligences who evolved around other stars could just as easily achieve the same level of sophistication. Given that some of them may have already reached that stage, and even surpassed it, it certainly is not unreasonable to think they may have already accomplished this feat, are even now traveling among the stars in asteroid ships, colony ships, if you will.

What's more, as our technology grows, we are capable of doing more and more. Is it then unreasonable to assume alien species might also evolve in their technological capabilities the same way, as well? If so, couldn't they hollow out even larger things than mere asteroids? Eventually, wouldn't moons be another way to go?

Why would a species want to go to such an extreme effort? That is a question that must be answered. Well, we've already demonstrated with our current capabilities of hollowing out asteroids, that such habitats would almost naturally have an urge to migrate to the edge of our solar system, to those places where resources are plentiful to sustain them, and so to easily create more of themselves.

We've also demonstrated there is no reason why they should stop at the edge of our solar system. Since they are self-contained habitats, they could just as easily travel through interstellar regions, as "generational ships" to the nearest star systems, and then beyond as being preferable to just orbiting forever around our sun at an extreme distance from it, until all resources are depleted there. Why would they do this, leave the solar system? Because they would be capable of doing it, that's why.

What would be their motivation? Well, we've already mentioned some. New resources, freedom from control of Earth perhaps, and sheer curiosity as to what may lie "out there," are among many other possible motivating factors. Survival as a species is another major one.

Unfortunately, besides just having expansion of their species and making their people safe from localized disasters, such as might occur here on Earth, there may be one other motivation, as well, that would drive them to do this.

This is a dark one. Other alien species, at least some of them, besides wanting to colonize the galaxy might also want to conquer it, make it theirs.

Regrettably, this is a possibility that simply cannot be overlooked. We can only hope this isn't the case with regard to us and any of those "others" who might visit us, but who knows?

So in this chapter we have asked the question of why someone would hollow out a moon or in our case, an asteroid. It seems there is a great motivation for us to do so. And if that motivation applies to us, it is only reasonable to assume it applies to other intelligent species, as well. As the old saying goes, "what is sauce for the goose is sauce for the gander," even alien "ganders."

If there are a multitude of intelligent races out there in the galaxy, then we have no reason to believe we have a monopoly on curiosity and developing technology. That would be an arrogant assumption in the extreme on our part to think so.

Chapter Conclusion. Therefore, we must conclude some other alien species have also happened on the idea of hollowing out asteroids and/or moonlets and moons. The idea just makes eminent sense. It is a practical solution to the survival of any species. It is a way to travel to the stars without having to have faster-than-light capabilities, which may be impossible anyway. It is a way for people to explore the universe without families having to be separated from each other.

And most of all, it is simply a safer way for a species to live. In our own created worlds we will simply be much safer than we could be on the surface of any planet, including this Earth. And, it is a logical way for any species that wants to explore the universe to do so. We want to. Why shouldn't others want the same thing?

Moreover, we've demonstrated that diasporas of alien races, by using hollow-out asteroids and such, may be the norm, a part of almost any civilization's progression. The galaxy may be full of such civilizations.

So it is likely there are hollowed out asteroids and or moonlets or moons "out there." In this chapter, we have demonstrated that it is hardly an unreasonable idea that such should exist, and so probably do exist.

CHAPTER 16
More On What's In A Hollow Moon

Of course, the next question has to be, what's inside a hollow Moon? Well, to a large extent, we may have already just answered that in the last chapter. We could assume, based on the previous chapter, any such hollow moon, regardless of its size, whether relatively small as in an asteroid, or as large as our neighboring sister world, the Moon, would have to have a self-sustaining population. This automatically presupposes it has a self-sustaining closed ecological system, as well, at least for the most part.

There might well be things it has to obtain elsewhere, things that over long periods of time it may not be able to produce on its own. These may include, but not be limited to, fuel sources and other resources to help sustain life and their level of technology.

Why do we make this caveat? Well, over the truly long-term it might be very hard to create a permanently self-sustaining ecosystem. There is always some "leakage" from most such systems, even the one here on Earth. Even our planet is losing some of its atmosphere to space and just as Mars lost most of its air over the eons. Nothing is forever. So even such hollowed-out worlds would need exterior resources to some degree throughout their lifespans, however long those lifespans may be, in order to supplement their needs.

Moreover, the lifespans of such inside-out worlds would depend upon the viability of the intelligences that occupy them. Retrograde or decaying civilizations, or cultures might actually lose the capability of sustaining their habitats over time. Alternatively, long expeditions through interstellar space might exhaust their resources, just as they might with hollowed-out asteroids we propose humans could create. If this is so, then they would have to stop at other stellar systems to "refuel," as it were, to restock.

So, we can assume in a hollowed-out moon, there would have to be some sort of permanent resident population. What state it might be in is a matter of conjecture. It could be in a state of high efficiency, sophistication, and technological superiority. It would certainly seem to have started out that way, just in order to create such a thing and start on its travels.

However, over millennia, or even millions of years, this state of affairs might change, and change for the worse. In that case, such a civilization may lose the capability of maintaining its environment efficiently. Such intelligences might have to resort to obtaining outside resources, for whatever reasons mentioned above. They might have to resort to something else, as well. A retrograde civilization inside of the Moon might have to resort to cannibalization of its habitat.

We're not talking about the "people" eating each other here. We're talking about them having to use up some of the material of the moon they inhabit, in order to continue to survive, to find the necessary resources, such as metals, energy sources and/or volatiles.

What are we saying here? Well, there is no guarantee that just because a civilization has reached the capability of inhabiting the inside of the Moon, of hollow it out for that purpose, that it will always maintain this capability. After all, as the saying goes, "life is change." We are simply saying that such change may not always be for the better.

So multiple possible scenarios for what might be inside a hollow Moon exist. These include, but may not be limited to:

1. A highly advanced species with amazing technological capabilities and powers.

2. A retrograde culture or decaying civilization that has lost much of its capabilities and must resort increasingly to obtaining the resources it needs from the "outside."

3. In this instance, the population of such an intelligent species might be falling in numbers.

4. And again in such an instance, it might also mean that such an intelligent species is becoming increasingly more desperate in its efforts to survive.

There is one other thing we haven't mentioned here and we have to, because it is terribly important. Although such hollowed-out habitats are a great way to survive and be safe, there is one other method of survival, as well, that is important. This is secrecy.

The fewer who know about the fact of your existence helps to ensure your survival. Given what we said earlier in this book, about the possible number of habitable worlds and therefore alien civilizations, one would assume some of them might be inimical in nature, quite possibly outright hostile.

There is the distinct possibility (probability?) at least some alien civilizations might be warlike, or actively hostile to other civilizations, predators. A great way to avoid having to deal with this is to exist inside a hollow world and keep your existence secret, at least for the most part.

Scientists now theorize (as also mentioned earlier in this book) that there may be more "rogue worlds" existing in interstellar space than around stars. So the civilization living inside of a hollowed-out habitat, if it wanted to hide, what better way to achieve this goal than to drift along in the interstellar void with such a plethora of empty worlds?

Again we resort to some old clichés here, such as "there is safety in numbers," and there certainly are, apparently, a tremendous number of rogue worlds "out there" and also, hiding, as being a tree in a forest. In this case, it'd be a case of not knowing which "tree" held life inside of it, as opposed to all the other lifeless "trees" out there, all those empty rogue worlds.

So the civilization existing inside of a hollowed-out moon might well end up by being incredibly secretive, even if such a civilization didn't start out that way in the beginning. Being so isolated, so literally internalized for so long, one could conceive of such a civilization becoming internalized in its very nature, its psyche, as well.

The entire world of this civilization would be the boundaries of the outer shell of its moon/asteroid, and if not in the beginning, then quite possibly becoming so over time. This may be even a natural outcome for such types of civilizations, this development of secretiveness and internalization.

So we certainly can't dismiss the idea civilizations existing for long periods of time inside of hollowed-out moons might well be very insular, much internalized, extremely introspective in nature, and highly secretive as a natural course. Over enough time, the secrecy might border on or become true xenophobia, their fear of anything foreign or alien.

This presents a dichotomy for them in such a case. Such worlds would have to travel to find resources, presumably to neighboring star systems and beyond, but at the same time, as they progressed, they would also become increasingly secretive and xenophobic in nature. This means that upon arriving in a new star system, they may still want to remain as hidden as possible to any of the "local species," that might exist there. In brief, this means they would want to remain hidden to the local inhabitants.

Such a situation also means one more thing. Hollowed-out moon/asteroid civilizations might also want to give up their wandering ways. As they became increasingly introverted and insular, they may decide the risk of entering other solar systems repeatedly is just too great. They might fear that sooner or later their luck would run out, and they could encounter an advanced hostile species by repeatedly doing this.

Therefore, if they found a solar system they liked, one that had plentiful resources for them for the perceivable future, they might just decide to take up permanent residence there. Again, this is a very reasonable assumption given the facts as stated herein.

Remember, this is all about long-term survivability. Those species wanting to endure over the eons would not want to shout their existence to the stars and invite the wrong attention, possibly exceedingly dangerous attention from hostile aliens. Quite the reverse would be true. They'd want just the opposite. After all, there is safety in anonymity.

Indeed, many futurists, scientists, and science fiction authors now say we probably should not be broadcasting the fact of our existence so freely into outer space with our radio waves. Since we don't know what's "out there," perhaps we should use a little more care, more discretion, be a little bit more inhibited and reticent about just how much we broadcast the fact that we are here.

So if we are already starting to feel this way about our place and long-term survivability in a potentially dangerous universe, it stands to reason hollowed-out moon civilizations might very well feel the same way. In fact, we'll go so far as to say here that we think this is probably very likely, much more so than not.

Again, it's all about long-term survivability of the species. You must do that which ensures your survival. And to be screaming out to possibly enemy aliens you are there, so come and attack us, probably just isn't a good idea for us humans, any more than it would be for those residing inside of a hollowed-out moon.

Chapter Conclusion. So again, what might we find in a hollowed-out moon? What might be hiding there? Well, by our standards, probably a highly advanced species. It may also well be a highly self-protected species, and one with strong tendencies of being xenophobic, having fear of anything foreign or alien to them.

Such a species might also be retrograde, decaying from within, and so be even more xenophobic as a result. This also means, however, that despite this xenophobia, they may be faced with the need to look "outside" of their world for the resources necessary for their continued survival. And this is their conundrum, the very dichotomy of their existence, not wanting to deal with anything "outside" of themselves, but having no choice but to do so.

Why is this last point important to us? Well we think that much is rather obvious. Despite their capabilities, despite the technology, such species would be strongly affected by their perspective on things with regard to the universe and others residing in it. This means that any hollowed-out world near us could very well harbor a species, one heavily colored by this viewpoint, and so it would materially and deeply affect the way they would tend to deal with us. And therein lies our problem.

You see, we might not be treated by them with great kindness or welcomed by them as being their space brothers/sisters. They might even look upon us with revulsion, xenophobic dislike developed over millennia, and so possibly even outright hostility.

If this last is the case, then we do have some problems, especially if there happens to be a hollowed-out moon near us. Don't we? But more on this later. For now, let's turn to a possible scenario as an example of just what might be the case with hollowed-out moons in our own solar system.

CHAPTER 17

Was Mars A Failed Experiment?

Within the last months, the Martian Rovers, those stalwart little machines, have reported they have detected no sign of methane in the areas they've searched on Mars. This is significant because methane is a byproduct of life, meaning living organisms. Without it, the prospects for finding anything alive on Mars today are diminished.

Conversely, the same Rovers have shown there was water on Mars in the past and a significant amount of it. By this, we mean actually free-flowing water, not in the form of ice, or locked up in rocks (although there is some of that still, even now). Scientists readily admit this would or could have supported microbial life in the distant past, if such existed then, or perhaps even more.

Therefore, as we've remarked earlier, the possibility for life having existed on Mars in the past, the chances of it are very good. Now we mentioned earlier about the Moon Phobos possibly being hollow. If you remember, Phobos is one of two moons, the other one being Deimos, but it is the moon, Phobos, that some scientists have conjectured may be hollow. It is also conjectured by many scientists that both moons may be captured asteroids.

What if both things are true? What if Phobos is a captured asteroid and it is hollow? Scientists say it can't be solid, must at least be "porous" have "voids" or "caverns" in it. The chances of this occurring by accident seem improbably low that both things should occur, accidental capture of the moon by Mars, and capturing a hollow one at that.

There is something else strange about Phobos, besides this "porous" or hollow aspect, and the fact of the odd monolith on it. There are also "grooves," as NASA scientists call them. "Grooves" is not a term usually applied to something created by natural forces. Yet the term "grooves" precisely describes these strange markings on Phobos.

And if it is hollow, and our Moon is, as well, at least to some extent, then one has to wonder why two worlds, one which may have once harbored life, and the other which still does, both possibly have hollow moons circling them. This just seems much too coincidental to seem likely, to be just a chance event, the result of merest coincidence.

Again, we can't understate this: it would seem just too unusual two worlds, both of which either have life on them, or had it in the past, should both have hollow moons.

So, given the premise the Martian moon, Phobos, may be hollow, and Mars may once have sustained life, if not on the scale that our planet does, we come to an intriguing summation of the evidence so far. Moreover, we suggest what we feel may be a very reliable scenario.

Mind you, this is just a scenario, not a fact, but it might well be true, or least to a large extent, since we base it on the available evidence we have a compiled here in this book so far.

SCENARIO: Based on many scientists' belief there could be billions of Earthlike planets in our galaxy alone and many of these could well harbor life, some with intelligent life, so we can reasonably and safely assume that alien races exist.

1. Rise of Alien Technology. Given many scientists now consider this a reasonable premise, we can logically move to the next step without fear of going astray. As we mentioned at the beginning of this book, it is also eminently reasonable to assume some of these intelligent races came into being long before we did. This means they would have reached our stage of technology perhaps ages before we have.

It is also reasonable to assume, therefore, at some point they would have surpassed us in their capabilities. This could have taken place any time, even billions of years ago, since our universe is almost fourteen billion years old and our solar system is a latecomer on the scene.

2. The Creation of Hollow Worlds. With their technological capabilities, many of those alien races may well have decided that for the sake of survival of the species, it would be best for some of them to "set sail" as it were, by utilizing asteroids, moonlets, or moons. If only for exploration, these would make sense, and just as Carl Sagan said, good economic sense, rather than building metal ships.

These asteroids, moons, or moonlets they would then hollow out, even as we are now capable of hollowing out asteroids with our own technology of today. These habitats, in the interior of such celestial bodies, would as we mentioned earlier, provide intelligent species with habitable space, a lot more safety and security than they would have on an alien planet's surface. This would almost certainly help to ensure the survival of their species, but would also allow them easier access to resources and maximum mobility, as well.

3. The Alien Diaspora—The First Wave. With regard to easy access to resources, and just as we would find to be so, the best and most readily obtained resources would be not involve the costly effort of going down into the gravity wells of planets. Nor would it require a vast expenditure then to raise such resources up from those planets' surfaces.

No, just as we would find this too expensive and too difficult to do too often, so would they. Logically and demonstrably, rather they would seek out and obtain what they need from other sources, sources in the form of other asteroids, comets, and plutons which have little or no gravity wells at all and therefore are no problem to access, and so would require little expenditure on the part of the aliens to mine them.

This means, if their solar systems evolved even partially the way ours has done and according to the laws of physics in general, then there comets and plutons would be at the outer edge of their solar systems, and far from their primary star, just as ours are.

The result would be in the First Wave of the alien diaspora. There would be a general migration away from the center of the solar system to its extreme edges and toward those plentiful supplies of easily obtained resources there.

4. The Alien Diaspora—The Second Wave. Now, based on our very logical deductions, which required no great leaps of imagination at all, but rather are based pretty much on available evidence, we have our alien races now residing at the edges of their solar systems. They now inhabit the interiors of asteroids and/or larger bodies.

They are in the outermost region of their own solar system, where it is easy to "refuel," as it were, or to put it more layman's terms, "to tank up." What do they do next? Well, there is nothing in the interior of their solar system they need. They no longer rely on their sun's energy, for example. So what's holding them there?

The answer is remarkably self-evident. Nothing. Just as someone might stand on the beach at the edge of the water, and there is a tremendous urge for them to dip their toe into that water, so too, would alien races want to dip their toes into interstellar space. They would have legitimate and very strong reasons to do so. For one thing, sooner or later they're going to use up those resources where they are, however plentiful they may be they are still finite.

Furthermore with such plentiful resources, there is little doubt the number of habitats would multiply accordingly. Moreover, the aliens are no more an exception to the Malthusian Principle than any other species, intelligent or otherwise, would be.

The more plentiful the supply of resources, the more they would multiply.

Eventually the population would outstrip the available resources, and if they want to avoid a major catastrophe in the form of a population collapse, it would have to go elsewhere to find more assets, or cut drastically back in size.

We're already facing the same problem on Earth, and obviously our answer isn't to cut back in population growth. So what alternative do they have but to start seeking elsewhere for more resources?

This would result in several things. The first is, it would add pressure for those asteroid and/or moonlet ships to begin voyages into interstellar space. The second is that while this process was going on, it would give impetus to accelerating their technological capabilities.

Just as our world was on the edge of mass starvation and famine because a lack of food supplies in the 1960s, and then used technology to come up with the "Green Revolution" to save itself, so too, would such a thing happen with the aliens. As the saying goes, "necessity is the mother of invention." This would hold just as true for aliens as it does for us.

In other words, there would be strong reasons for them to advance their technology even further than what ours currently is. They would have to do this just in order to meet the necessities they would be facing under such harsh Malthusian circumstances.

And finally, remember what we said about them tending to become insular, isolated societies as time went by, complete unto themselves, and increasingly more introspective in their perspectives? Remember how we also said their xenophobic tendencies might begin to grow stronger, become a major factor in their viewpoint of things?

This could easily reach the stage where even each asteroid or moonlet (moon?) Would want to have little or nothing to do with any of the others, even though they're still of the same species. Rather than have conflicts or go to war, why not just sail away into the infinite void of interstellar space and so survive that way?

All this would provide powerful reasons, potent motivations for such alien races to begin the voyage into deep interstellar space. And here we haven't even mentioned the fact such a tactic would help to ensure the longevity and survivability of their species as a whole. It would be very hard for another hostile alien race to hunt them down and destroy them all, when hundreds, thousands or, perhaps even millions of asteroids are scattered throughout the galaxy.

Our conclusion is it would almost be inevitable for an alien race, unless for some reason it had massive differences in its psychological makeup from us, to begin spreading out to the stars in such a fashion. An important thing to remember here is it does not require super technologies or even faster-than-light speeds in order to do this. Also remember, this could have happened for some races a very long time ago, even before our planet was born. This is an important point to think of for later.

5. The Alien Diaspora—The Third Wave. Now we come to the third wave of the alien diaspora. This is where the enclosed habitats of the aliens would reach the first neighboring solar systems. Here, they would have two choices: the first is they could remain there indefinitely, on a very long-term basis. This might be true especially if the solar system was not inhabited by any other intelligent species. After all, this would give them unfettered access to the entire system's resources without fear.

However, the habitats may launch from their home system as huge fleets, there being safety in numbers. If most of the habitats of any given fleet arrived in the solar system, or even several fleets arrived there, then again, there will be competition for the available resources. This may not be a problem in the beginning. But eventually, sooner or later, it will be, especially if the habitats reproduce, create more of themselves.

This would seem likely if there were available resources to do so. The alternative would be to practice population control. This would seem unlikely to us, since with an apparently inexhaustible supply of resources in the galaxy, by simply going to them, they wouldn't have to exercise such limitations, restrictions on their populations. Moreover, the greater the population, the greater would be the long-term viability and so the survivability of the species as a whole. Again, there is safety in numbers.

However, sooner or later, given all this, there would be the same motivations to move on yet again. This time, there might be newly created habitats that would go on, as well. Thus, we begin the third wave of the alien diaspora. From the star systems adjacent to their home system, many of these worldlet communities would again set out to the stars nearest to the ones of the system they now occupied. And in all probability there would be even more such habitats to travel along with them by this point.

Eventually, some of them would come to our star system. This may have happened long ago. And a world that might have once harbored life, even only on the microbial level, would have attracted their attention. This world could very well have been Mars in its earlier phase of existence, many millions of years ago, possibly even billions.

One or more of these habitats may have arrived in our solar system. Even now, we can't be sure if there was more than one, despite the fact we have some evidence that two habitats may be here, an old one around Mars, and one circling the Earth now in the form of the Moon.

Why do we say this? Well, if only one habitat made it to our solar system, it would seem natural for it to take up orbit around Mars first. We say this, because Mars is on the outer edge of the Asteroid Belt, an area with a vast supply of resources for the alien-occupied asteroid. And again, there would be attraction to a world that had some sort of life upon it, if only for scientific reasons, curiosity on the part of interstellar aliens. Perhaps such beings even contemplated colonizing Mars.

However, we think this would be an aborted scenario, if so. The aliens would know, just as we do now, that Mars would be incapable of sustaining life to any relevant degree for the long haul, or to any great degree. The world is just too small, the gravity too low to sustain an atmosphere for the longer term. The solar wind, in the form of radiation, would then sterilize the surface of the planet, and just as it seems to have done. And Mars is probably a bit too large of a world to conveniently move around as one would an asteroid, moonlet, or moon. So the urge to colonize Mars might simply not have been there.

Besides this, the aliens would have traveled for perhaps countless generations aboard their habitat. They would have had plenty of time to develop their technologies further in order to sustain them. At the same time, they also might well have grown ever more xenophobic in the process. Where microbial life on Mars might not make them feel too threatened, any more advanced form just might.

Why do we push this aspect of the xenophobia with regard to the aliens? Because we think, based on available evidence, and if the aliens are at all like us, they would have this trait and in abundance. This is just a matter of an acquired trait even if they didn't start out with it, just from being isolated for so long.

Even so, it's also quite possible being so alone for such a very long time in the depths of interstellar space for countless generations that this might make them want to seek out others all the more. However, this must be tempered with the fear of meeting up with competitors, fierce competitors, at that.

Is this fear justified? Yes, definitely it would be. Somewhere "out there," a species or species must exist that would be quite willing to destroy others so that they alone dominate. Moreover, it is likely there could very well be many such aggressive species, hundreds, thousands, perhaps even millions or more of them, given the size of our universe and that it may be infinite.

This would have to be the case, given the laws of probability. I don't think our alien friends would be unaware of this. They certainly would understand the laws of probability just as well as we do, if not more so.

Although the universe is vast, competition could still be great for resources. If each race creates habitats which then spread out and create more habitats which then spread out and create even more habitats, ad infinitum, it wouldn't take long for just one species to fill an entire galaxy to have explored and colonized the whole thing. It is estimated (under ideal circumstances) that one species could colonize the entire galaxy in relatively short order.

Again, considering the universe is almost 14 billion old, that's less than a second in the cosmic scale of time when compared to those eons that have already passed. Even under much less ideal conditions, it is estimated one species could occupy the entire galaxy in less than one million years. In other words, this could already have been done repeatedly and long before Earth even formed.

If one race can do this why not all the others? If some of them are aggressively hostile and/or deadly, and spreading like a decimating plague upon the galactic scene, then just becoming xenophobic through isolation wouldn't be the only reason for aliens to shun others. It could well be a very practical survival option for them to keep on living. At the very least, they could exercise great caution in their dealings with other species.

They might even go one step further. They might want to form allies, or failing that, create them. At the very least, they might decide they could use such junior-partner species, created or otherwise, to act as deceptions, distractions, for such aggressive species to focus on, rather than themselves.

While they remain hidden in the depths of interstellar space, it could well be other species created by them could well be broadcasting their existence merrily and mindlessly without thought to the universe. In other words, our alien nomads might even create or use other species as a diversionary tactic to save themselves from predator species. Younger races, as it were, might be thrown to galactic wolves.

This raises an interesting question; are we such a species? Are we being set up as some cosmic mousetrap? Could our "so-called" alien space brothers be setting us up? It could be. The purpose would be to protect themselves, to ensure their survivability, by distracting, diverting possible enemies toward us, rather than them.

They might even actually be creating a trap. If hostile intelligences then decided to attack us, they could remain hidden quietly nearby to initiate a counterstrike or leave when it's all over and the enemy have departed.

Does this scenario seem incredibly far-fetched? Perhaps, at first glance it would. However, we have the laws of probability on our side. And according to those laws and based on what we see on our own planet, with survival of the fittest, the constant war and competition for resources by all the species on our Earth, the death struggles that ensue, and the inevitable extinctions, why wouldn't this be true for the alien races, as well? Again, according to the laws of probability, it "probably" would be the case.

But, you say, the aliens would be more advanced than us, would have grown in their ideas of morality, and so would be peaceful, become our "space brothers?" Think again. Although some might choose this path, and it would be a dangerous one for them, because sooner or later they might chance upon one of those hostile alien races, many others, would still opt to keep as low a profile as possible as a survival strategy.

They would not see other intelligent species as friends. Far more likely, given the circumstances, the competitive hunt for resources, etc., quite the reverse should be true. At the very least, other alien species would be competitors. At the very worst, they might be genocidal beings, intent on surviving at all costs, including the destruction of possible competitors. Such is nature. Such is how life is on our world right now.

The universe may seem to be a peaceful place, just as a lush garden might appear to an onlooker who didn't know better. But examine that garden more closely. Insects eat the plants. Other insects eat those insects. Birds and other small creatures then eat those insects. And other creatures eat those animals in turn. And so it goes and continues to go. Even members of the same species compete with each other for survival.

What appears to be a lush garden is in reality, a jungle, and a jungle in every sense of the term, even the worst sense. In order for life to flourish, it must eat other life. Why would we have any rational reason to believe this stops on our planet and goes no further? In all "probability," and unfortunately, it probably does.

Logically, and this is using sheer logic, wherever there is life, there must be a struggle for life, competition, and resulting deaths. There must be competition in order for any one species to survive. And the longer that species survives, probably the better it gets at destroying its competition. So keep this in mind the next time you think that aliens are our "space brothers."

And if you think we're not that way as a species, then check out the number of wars, battles, revolutions, and civil disturbances going on at any one time around our planet. They are endless and they are numerous. And sadly, they never cease. People always seem to be killing other people around our world.

Why then, should we expect an alien species to be any different, especially when what it faces is even a far more hostile situation and on a much greater scale, one literally the size of the universe itself?

No, given our own planet, its own history of struggle for life, and the resulting extinction of species here (it is estimated by scientists that 99.9 percent of all species that have ever lived on Earth are now extinct), we must assume this is the way it works elsewhere in the universe, too. If we are not unique, as most scientists now say, then this would just stand to reason. It's a cold, brutal sort of reasoning, but it's probably true.

So our aliens would definitely suffer from xenophobia and with darn good reason. It's the best way to survive. Yet, as we will discuss a bit later in this book, there would be a need for some interaction with other species. That, too, would be part of the survival strategy.

In any case, Mars was a failed experiment with regard to life as we know it. The aliens, no less intelligent than us, and perhaps more so, given the amount of time they had to evolve, would undoubtedly come to the same conclusion. That is, if they weren't instrumental in the destruction of life on Mars, which also could be. Killing young species off is a way to avoid trouble with them later on, as they develop.

Either way, our solar system still would have vast resources for them. They would be in no hurry to move on. So why not stay for a while, and perhaps focus on another planet that might have life on it, see what happens there, and in the process improve their environment, as well. After all, advanced as they are, they would have nothing to fear from a primitive species, right?

However, after all that time in deep space, their habitat by then must have been well-worn. Why not create a new one? And with their technologies, their ever-growing capabilities, why not a bigger and better one?

Why not something the size of our Moon? Furthermore, why not position it in orbit around a planet that already has or shows the prospects of developing life? Certainly, for them, there would be much to learn there.

Thus ends our scenario. A hollow moon, our Moon as we think of it, takes up orbit around the Earth sometime in our past. It may have happened near the beginning of our recorded past, or before the beginning of civilization, based on those records saying there was a time when there was no Moon in the sky. It may even have happened in the far, the very remote past, perhaps when

Earth was still in its formative stages. With the available evidence we have, we simply can't be certain of this. We can only make educated guesses.

Chapter Conclusion. Yes, this is just a scenario, one of possibly many, but it could very well be a most likely one. If intelligence forms much the same way throughout the galaxy in the universe as we did, then undoubtedly, it would have the same basic motivations, the need to survive, to expand and grow. Curiosity would be another factor. Fear would be one, as well, and it would undoubtedly exhibit itself in the form of xenophobia, just as it does here on Earth in certain countries.

For instance, the United Kingdom has long been accused over the centuries of being xenophobic. Some psychologists have even argued the English have had such restrictive quarantine measures for animals in the very recent past because of this, as a manifestation of that xenophobia. Up until recently, and even now to a great extent, many English think of anyone from anywhere else, or anything for that matter that does not come from England, as being "foreign." This despite the fact the United Kingdom is now an integral part of greater Europe, and less than 30 miles have separated it from Europe (by the English Channel), throughout its history.

We're not picking on the English here, either. Many countries experience a fear of the foreign, and suffer from some form of xenophobia to a greater or less extent. The United States, for example, between World War I and World War II experienced a strong xenophobia, and became very isolationist.

Whereas the English only had a narrow channel between them in Europe, we had two oceans to safeguard us. For a whole generation we thought that would be enough and that we didn't need anyone else. Of course, we were wrong. The world still intrudes whether we wanted it to not. The same would be true for aliens.

So there we have it. Mars was a failed experiment, and the new arrivals decided to better their circumstances and move on. They might have decided to take up orbit around another planet in perhaps a new habitat, one which was much bigger, and could provide them with the resources they might need for another interstellar journey a very long duration, if necessary. Alternatively, maybe they just have different-sized habitats, big and small ones as a matter of course. We would. We could utilize Ceres, a dwarf planet in the Asteroid Belt down to very small asteroids, if we so choose to create our own diaspora.

But the point is; it may be a simple case of, as the line goes, "they came, they saw, and they conquered," so to speak. After all, how could a young race such as ourselves stop an ancient and technologically powerful one from drifting in from "out there" and taking charge, not only of our solar system, but perhaps of us, as well? Does their habitat now loom close in our night sky? Do they rule that night sky, as well?

CHAPTER 18

Our Moon, An Alien Hollow World?

What does this mean for us, exactly? Well, the Moon could truly be an alien world in our skies. As shown much earlier in this book, there seems to be good evidence this just might well be the case. And one more time, and we repeat this for emphasis here, reputable scientists came up with this theory and not us!

If that's the case, then our Moon wasn't always here. If this is so, then it may not always be here in the future. If it arrived, as some historical records seem to indicate, just a mere 11,000 years ago (give or take a couple thousand years), then why wouldn't they be expected to also leave again at some point? Our Moon may just be a temporary visitor.

Just the implications of that alone are stunning. We definitely think of the Moon as "ours," of always having been here, and for the long foreseeable future, always continuing to be here.

And where Mars might have been a failed experiment in life and so a possible disappointment for the aliens, the Earth is not. Our planet teems with living things.

Again, is this all wild conjecture on our part? No, we don't think so. We are assuming certain things, but those assumptions are based on solid scientific facts, on the evidence of the multiple numbers of planets discovered throughout our galaxy.

Our assumptions are also based on other evidence provided by scientists, reputable scientists, and many of them. We aren't making this stuff up. It's real. Our conjectures may be incorrect, but the basis for them is well-grounded in science.

Finally, our reasonable conjecture, the scenario in the last chapter, is not just some wild fantasy in our part. The scenario is based:

1. Various anomalies in the orbit of the Moon.

2. The odd makeup of our Moon. This includes not only the strange elements involved in its composition, elements that should not be there, the thickness of the crust being greater on one side of the Moon than the other, the relative lack of mares on the far side of the Moon, as well as such oddities, as the Moon "ringing like a bell," that has been struck. There are many other things as well, such as moonquakes that can't be accounted for, as well.

3. The (so far) inexplicable nature of the Moon's origin.

4. Centuries of transient lunar phenomena, and other strange things about our Moon.

5. Recent data concerning the probability of thousands, perhaps millions, even billions of other Earth like planets just in our galaxy alone.

6. The probability that life might exist on those planets, as well as intelligent life.

7. Reasonable assumptions that other intelligent species might achieve the same levels of technology that we have, if not more, given the amount of time that has already passed in our universe.

8. Use of the Laws of Probability, and Statistics.

9. The idea other alien races would be just as capable of moving out in colonizing waves, successive diasporas, if you will, throughout our galaxy.

10. The rationale for such species developing (if they hadn't already) a strong sense of xenophobia.

11. The rationale that such species would also develop as many strategies for long-term survival as possible.

Chapter Conclusion. If all this seems extreme to you, we can only repeat once more, you must remember, we aren't the ones who came up with the idea of a hollow Moon, other Earthlike worlds that might have life upon them, or any of these ideas/scenarios. Scientists did. We are only compiling them, attempting to come to some conclusions about it all.

As for the idea of alien diasporas, although conjecture on our part, it certainly is not in the realm of fantasy by any means. This idea is grounded solidly in facts, what's actually possible for us to do right now, ourselves, the basic urge of any living species to want to survive, to expand its population, and increase the odds that it will continue to survive, as well as the instinct to explore, be curious.

After all, isn't that what evolution is all about, to slowly evolve better means of sustaining a species, allowing for its continued existence, to develop strategies and various methods for its survival? Moreover, as far as there being an alien species out there, again it is not us who say this is a probability, but scientists. We certainly didn't come up with this idea on our own.

And the idea of an alien diaspora is also based on a very solid reality, that even with today's technology; we have the capability of doing these ourselves, and probably eventually will. The same imperatives, the same needs for increased access to resources, population pressures, curiosity, and the urge to survive will motivate us. This is just as surely as it motivates other intelligent species throughout the universe. The diaspora idea is further supported by the idea that the resources for such habitats would lie in the greatest quantity at the extreme edges of our solar system, a natural "jumping off point," and so they would lie at the extreme edges of other ones, as well.

Furthermore, our theory is based that on the Principle of Malthusian Economics, that sooner or later, those habitats must launch themselves into interstellar space, if only for the need of more resources to support their burgeoning populations. Either that or they would have to face famines and ultimate failure for their civilizations.

One can't forever ignore the concept of the so-called "Malthusian catastrophe." This simply states populations grow based on the resources available to them. Sooner or later, all populations reach a tipping point, when the resources diminish and/or the population grows beyond the available resources. A "crash," or "catastrophe" then ensues, and the population falls suddenly and dramatically.

One can only circumvent this by finding new resources or better utilization of old resources, and even this last can't be done indefinitely to sustain an ever-growing population. Such human habitats in asteroids would have no choice but to join a diaspora in search of new resources. The same would most likely apply to aliens, as well.

So these aren't just wild assumptions on our part. We have done our best to base them on the available facts, evidence, and surmises of mainstream astronomers, and other researchers. These are reputable people, and people of note, as with Carl Sagan, Isaac Asimov, and other such noteworthy individuals, as examples.

However, let us move on, because there is more. There is still the matter of those aliens. Just who are they, why are they here, and what do they want. How long might they have been here?

These are all important issues for us as humans and we shall try to answer them here. Why are they so important? Well, if our Moon is hollow, then it might just well be that aliens not only rule the sky. It may even be they rule us. We will discuss this more in the next chapters.

CHAPTER 19

Is There A "No Trespassing" Sign On The Moon?

"Signs, signs, signs, everywhere a sign…" Remember those lyrics from that old song? Well, they might even apply to the Moon. Why do we say this? Well, because something strange seems to have been going on for the last four decades or so.

In the late 1950s, all through the 1960s and into the very early 1970s, the "space race," as all the news media referred to it, was in full swing. Kids wanted to grow up to be astronauts. I and my friends all had visions of lunar bases and manned expeditions to Mars. All this was fed, magnified and exaggerated by the fact of the Space Race.

And since as most historians point out, the Space Race was a direct outgrowth of the Cold War with which America was so deeply involved with the Soviet Union, one would have expected it to have continued. If putting a man on the Moon by 1969 was an absolute must, it certainly seemed there was enough motivation to continue the space program full tilt, because the Cold War hadn't ended, and in fact had heated up by the mid-1970s.

Yet a curious thing happened. Despite the fact the Cold War still persisted and even, if anything, worsened throughout the 70s and 80s, the Space Race, for all practical purposes, came to a dead end. The last manned Apollo mission to the Moon took place in

1972, just three years after the first humans, Americans, landed for the first time on our celestial neighbor.

And that was it. Suddenly, not only America, but everyone seemed to have lost interest in the Moon. And it would seem all too swiftly.

The Russians who had been vying with us to get there never made it. At least, they didn't make it in respect of being able to putting one of their own cosmonauts on the Moon. And America, although we had barely scratched the lunar surface, did the same. The most we managed was the rare or occasional satellite in lunar orbit. The Russians had a probe or two, as well, but that was it! It was all over—done.

Instead, NASA suddenly shifted its attention to putting a space station, the Skylab, in near orbit around the Earth. Again, we remind you the Cold War was still in full swing. And it would be so for the better part of the next two decades, until the time of the collapse of the Soviet Union on December 26, 1991.

So a Cold War that had started immediately after World War II, and gone on for over twenty years, still had about another twenty years to go. Yet again, the Space Race abruptly came to an end for all real considerations long before that time. Suddenly, and despite ever intensifying rivalry with the Soviet Union, the urge for us and them, both sides to show dominance in space, we went from traveling from a quarter of the million miles each way to the Moon, to just a mere few hundred above the Earth's surface.

Why did it all so abruptly cease? Those who argue the end of the Cold War was responsible for the end of the Space Race are simply and blatantly wrong. The Cold War had not ended. Under President Ronald Reagan it amped up considerably and this was right near the end of the lifespan of the Soviet Union. We were spending billions upon billions of dollars annually to compete with Russia at the time, were even researching a "Star Wars" defense style program.

Others argue it was the extreme cost of the Space Race program that ended the trips to the Moon. And yes, NASA always struggled with its budget and Congress over it. But this was nothing new. Right from the start they had such budgetary fights. Nothing had really changed in this regard.

The Apollo program at its peak was estimated to cost the United States just about $24 billion. This came to about 2.7% of the national budget at the time for the manned expeditions. The total cost of NASA at the time was about 5.3% of our national budget. This was nothing compared to what was being spent on the Cold War and our military rivalry with the Soviet Union. Even then, as the NASA budget percentage dropped, our defense budget rose ever more steeply and way out of proportion to the cuts at NASA.

So let's pretend for a moment that maybe it was the cost of the program that curtailed our trips to the Moon so suddenly. Maybe, the Skylab program was a much better bang for the buck?

Well, let's see; the cost of the Skylab program in 2010 dollars was equal to about $11 billion or $2.6 billion at the time of its launch in 1973 dollars. This was just for the launch of the original basic module, without any of the additions that have been going on ever since. They've continued to cost much more.

It is estimated the average cost of a launch of a rocket to send people up to the Skylab, and/or supplies, runs about $435 million for each one. This does not take into account the cost of the materials and supplies on board these rockets. Moreover, the entire cost of the space shuttle program, which was principally used to resupply the Skylab for a very long time, is estimated to be at about $200 billion. That's $200 billion, folks!

What is the total cost of the Skylab program, considering all of this? Well, let's just say it far outstripped the cost of the Apollo manned mission programs to the Moon. So if Skylab cost so much more than the Apollo program did, then we can't really believe it was the cost that caused America, and so NASA, to cease sending people to the Moon. The Moon program was a lot cheaper by comparison!

And yet, still, the Space Race was over. Not only did America not seem interested in the Moon any longer to any real extent, but neither, oddly, did the Soviets, or anyone else for that matter. Nobody.

If one believed in conspiracy theories, one might really wonder at this. Why, all of a sudden, something that was the most important thing of the world for humanity to achieve suddenly wasn't worth bothering to continue at all, not in any way, shape, or real form, and not by anybody? How could attitudes have switched so abruptly? Why would they spend billions upon billions for intercontinental ballistic missiles, nuclear warheads, but suddenly a single rocket to the Moon was out of the question, cost-wise? Something seems very wrong there.

And no reasonable explanation that we've heard seems to exist to account for this sudden, and we mean sudden, change of direction. If rivalry was the cause of the Space Race, it was the Cold War that heated up that race to white-hot levels.

Then why did that Space Race suddenly stop, as if it had hit a brick wall, even though the Cold War ground on for years, almost two more decades? How could one explain the sudden cessation of the Apollo program, with the Skylab program in its totality, cost so much more? And in all that time, we never once tried to land anyone on the Moon again, even though our technology to do so increased virtually exponentially and was an already proven technology.

In case you aren't aware of it, it has now been FORTY YEARS since anyone has set foot upon the Moon. Soon, it will be half a century! We managed to make it there with 1960's technology, but we can't make it there much more easily and safely with Twenty-First Century technology? Again, something seems very wrong about that.

Of course, some argue the benefits/cost ratios simply weren't there. We weren't getting enough out of going to the Moon to make it worthwhile. Then one has to wonder, just exactly what have we achieved with the Skylab program with regard to such potential benefits? We hear about all sorts of experiments being conducted there all the time, and yet we hear about almost no results of these experiments, no concrete benefits at all. Can you name one, for instance, just one?

And really, for the most part, the experiments seem trifling in the extreme. Does it really take a $200 billion Skylab to see if plants will grow in freefall, or might a robotic space capsule have done the same thing far more cheaply? And if they can grow in freefall, does it really matter? We say this, because there seem to be no plans for any sort of manned expeditions to the Moon again, Mars, or beyond. So why do we need to know if plants will grow in outer space?

Yes apparently, they are conducting lots of experiments on board the Skylab. We just wonder why no positive and significant results from these experiments have been made public. After all, if our government and NASA made a point of doing this, wouldn't it help justify the tremendous cost of the Skylab to advertise such results? Yet, we see and hear almost nothing about them.

In fact, we hear far more about the results of the Hubble Space Telescope than we do about all of the experiments on Skylab combined. And some of those results have been fantastic. Would that we could say the same thing for Skylab, but we cannot.

So if it is a cost/benefits ratio that made Apollo an obsolete idea and so made Skylab a better option, we just don't see it. We don't see the results. We don't see any real positive benefits coming from Skylab. Show us the proof of this!

For all practical purposes, it just seems to be floating in orbit around the Earth snapping photographs and doing elementary-school-level experiments. As for photographs, the Hubble Telescope beats it by far. As for experiments, we find it hard to see how $200 billion was necessary to perform these that could have been done aboard the space shuttles just as easily.

There we have it. Suddenly, we stopped going to the Moon. For forty years nobody, not us, nor any other nation has been back, has set actual foot upon that world. All the explanations given to us simply don't seem to work when examined. They seem grossly inadequate. Moreover, they seem almost farcical. We find it hard anyone would even believe such explanations.

The strange part about all this is that it wasn't just the United States. Long before the collapse of the Soviet Union, almost twenty years ago, that country simply ceased trying to land anybody on the Moon. Europe hasn't tried at all.

Under the second President Bush, he did announce a plan to return to the Moon, but that seems to have come to nothing. In fact, it seemed a very lame program to begin with and never really intended even to get off the ground. Therefore, it comes across as almost a smoke screen ("Yeah, we're going back to the Moon, but not really…")

It's unlikely to ever even have reached a real planning stage to any degree as yet, and now another decade has passed. It was almost as if it was for public consumption, rather than for reality. In other words, perhaps it was just to keep us happy, and keep us from wondering why we weren't really going back to the Moon?

So we have a real mystery here. And the question increasingly being asked is: Why haven't we been back to the Moon? We don't even send robots, but we send them all the way to Mars, and not just once, but repeatedly? Very strange!

Well, the answer to our question might be simpler than we realize. Perhaps someone has placed a sort of celestial "No Trespassing" sign on our lunar neighbor. After all, if it isn't cost, technological capabilities, the lack of a Cold War, that caused us to stop going, then there don't seem to be a lot of other explanations left. What else could it be? Do we just suddenly not care about our nearest planetary neighbor? This would seem unlikely. The Moon, as with the tides for instance, has far more direct influence on us than Mars does. It's far closer than Mars.

All our dreams of space bases on the Moon, of lunar exploration, and then using that world as a stepping stone to Mars and the other planets, suddenly somehow ceased to be a possibility or probability. Instead, because of so-called cost factors as NASA tries to tell us, unmanned expeditions into deep space are a "better deal." Are they?

Or are they all that's left to us humans? Maybe, humanity isn't going to be allowed to be "out there" on the Moon? Maybe, we've been warned away. Otherwise, one has to ask the question, why haven't we been back, and why aren't we going back?

Yes, China seems to be planning a trip there, and let's hope that comes to fruition. They did send their Jade Rabbit, although that hasn't functioned well at all. Our program under President Bush certainly didn't, either. And yet, Rovers travel tens of millions of miles (versus just 230,000 or so miles to the Moon), and function perfectly fine for years on Mars!

Why not send some of those to the Moon, as well, if cost factors are such a consideration? How about just one? Why are we exploring everything but what's in our own immediate backyard? We send probes to Jupiter, Saturn, the moon, Titan, but not to our own Moon?

Chapter Conclusion. So just maybe, someone or some "thing" has warned us off the Moon. It would seem to have to be something like this; otherwise, there seems no rational explanation as to why we haven't been back in almost half a century. The Moon hasn't lost any of its allure. If anything, the number of mysteries concerning it hasn't lessened, but only has grown with the information we gathered from those original lunar landings.

We have more questions to answer now than when we started out. Yes, there definitely seems to be some sort of no trespassing zone when it comes to the Moon, or at least portions of it. One can only wonder why. Why can't we go back? Why don't we try to go back? What are we afraid of there? Is it because we've been warned not to?

CHAPTER 20
Who Warned Us Off The Moon?

Just who might occupy the Moon? Well, as this entire book has been trying to say, we think someone has inhabited the place. That much seems to be likely, at least. If they are, or have been there in the past, they must have stayed largely below the surface, although there is evidence that at times they have come out onto the exterior of the Moon, and may even have or once had bases on the surface. We refer you to Chapter Seven of this book with regard to evidence for this, the various statements by astronauts, etc., recordings, and photographs concerning this subject.

So let's try to answer the question of just who may be on the Moon a little more closely. We will give you a hint; it isn't us humans. Yes, we are talking about aliens, genuine aliens here. If any still wondered this, let us make that clear. But just who are they and why are they here? From where do they come? Well, there are several possibilities. We've already named the one we think the most likely, but let's go over the alternatives here just as a quick reminder:

1. The aliens are from our own solar system.

2. The aliens are from Earth, a different species from and hidden from us.

3. The aliens are from elsewhere, and by elsewhere we mean outside of our own solar system.

Let's take these one by one. First of all, could the aliens be from our own solar system? Yes, it is certainly conceivable they could be, but then one has to raise the question of precisely where have they come from. What planet in our solar system in particular could they have evolved on?

Well, if we base the concept of alien life forms as having to follow the same evolutionary rules as we have, and have come about from DNA, then that limits the possible origins. For instance, although there may be life on Jupiter, it certainly wouldn't be life as we know it. This would tend to rule out the other gas giants as possible origins for the aliens, as well.

Therefore, we can probably cross off Jupiter, Saturn, Neptune, and Uranus as possible home worlds for the aliens, because these are all gas giants. By the same token, we can probably rule out the Oort Cloud, as well as the Kuiper Belt. Again, although they may support some type of life, it could only be microbial, at best, or so different from us as to be unrecognizable as life, at least, as we know it.

Obviously, this now begins to define a limit, considerably narrows down where they could have come from within our solar system. We are just left with the more "rocky" worlds, of which our Earth is one, a few moons, and the asteroid belt.

The asteroid belt we can probably rule out, as well. Although there may be some sort of microbial life on such a protoplanet (an asteroid that didn't quite get to become a planet), as Ceres, which does seem to have a lot of fresh water for its size, if frozen, perhaps, for the most part, there is little chance of a highly-developed species evolving there. Smaller asteroids than Ceres simply don't have any atmospheres at all to speak of, or the right conditions for any sort of life, most likely.

Moreover, we can still and with some real degree of confidence, limit the possible origins of aliens even more. For example, it is just as unlikely life ever formed on Mercury or Venus, again at least, not life that we would recognize as such.

Certainly, we wouldn't find life with a technological sophistication and so intelligence.

The conditions on Venus, although an Earthlike planet in size, are just too extreme. The world has a crushing carbon dioxide atmosphere, equal in pressure at the surface to the depths of our deepest oceans. The average surface temperature is about 864°. This is equivalent to an oven set on the self-cleaning mode where it reduces all organic matter to a fine white ash. And this is all the time!

Mercury, a small rocky world, being so incredibly close to the sun, also is too extreme in conditions with regard to radiation, heat and, oddly, cold, as well. On the day side of the planet some metals would run as liquid rivers, so hot is the surface. Any life based on DNA would be sterilized, reduced to a fine ash. On the night side of the planet, the temperatures can drop toward absolute zero.

Nothing we know of could grow and evolve under such circumstances. Life, again, at least as we would know it, would have a very hard time gaining any foothold on that planet, and then surviving for any length of time afterwards. Again, the idea of a technologically advanced intelligent species evolving there is slim to none.

Well, we've now ruled out six of the eight planets in our solar system (not counting Pluto, once considered the ninth planet, but which has been declassified from this to being a mere pluton, and is far too cold to support life based on DNA, in any case). This leaves only our own Earth, Mars, and perhaps a couple of the moons of Jupiter and one of Saturn.

We will leave the Earth alone for the moment, since we intend to discuss that separately. Instead, we will focus on the moons.

As for the moons of Jupiter, there are two possibilities where life may be, even now. These are the moons Callisto and Europa. Although they have frozen surfaces, with impossibly harsh environments there for life, it is believed these moons likely have oceans beneath their radiated and icy crusts. These oceans, in all probability, are composed of liquid water, and so could support life.

The moon, Titan, a satellite of Saturn, might just manage some form of life, as well, although again, it might not be as we know life, being a world with a methane atmosphere and incredibly cold. Still, it's thought life formed on Earth in a similar sort of atmosphere, if warmer, so it is a possibility. But if it is life as we know it, it probably hasn't evolved into anything intelligent yet, if it exists at all.

Even so, Callisto and Europa do hold out the greatest hope there may be life somewhere else besides our Earth in our solar system. However, being worlds with oceans, if there is life there, and even if it had evolved intelligence, it would probably be an aquatic species in nature. If such an aquatic intelligence came to Earth, it would probably then be much more interested in our oceans then in our land masses.

Could there be such a species visiting our world, or even colonizing it without us even knowing it? Possibly. After all, numerous USOs (Unidentified Submerged Objects) have been sighted over the centuries. This is true even as far back as the time of Christopher Columbus and before. So we do know there are unidentified submerged objects coming and going from our waters.

Moreover, this is exactly what one would expect if an aquatic alien race was visiting or colonizing the Earth, or just setting up bases here. They would want to do so in those regions of Earth most like their home world, in this case, in the depths of our oceans. They would have to have developed a very different technology from our own, of course.

Our civilization is based on the invention of fire and its uses for various purposes. We use it for everything from forging metals to cooking our meals. It is highly unlikely an aquatic species would have developed a civilization based on that particular method, not when they live underwater.

So is such an aquatic race of aliens possible? Yes, we think it definitely is. Also, it's possible that such a species may be visiting or even setting up bases in our oceans? Yes, that too, is distinctly possible.

However, in such instances as this, we have to use the Principle of Occam's Razor. Since it would be harder (in our considered opinion) for an alien aquatic species to develop the type of technologies to travel through space, when they would develop (probably) without a concept of fire and so the ability to forge metals, for instance, then we have to go with the idea the aliens probably would not be aquatic in nature. This is not to say this isn't the case. We just think there is a more likely, simpler solution. One other thing; we haven't sighted any ships in or around these moons ever.

So to get back to our process of elimination, this just leaves us with Mars and Earth. We have robotic vehicles on Mars. As yet, we've seen no signs of life there, not even fossil evidence, although admittedly, our Rovers have only scratched at the tiniest portion of the planet's surface, and we mean surface. They can't drill very deep at all.

Even so, based on this evidence, at best, it seems we can only hope for the most primitive forms of life, microbial in nature, if any even of those still do survive there. For the surface seems to have been irradiated, sterilized by radiation from our sun and cosmic rays. So even if there is life there at all, it must be subterranean in nature.

This is a possibility, of course. But would there be any advanced life, intelligent forms still alive, if ever? Is there any evidence this possibility may be true? For example, have we seen any anomalies on Mars that might signify an intelligent species dwells within the planet, in caverns, perhaps?

In the past, some observers, including even in the nineteenth century did spot a few anomalies on that world, but our telescopes were far less powerful back then, and with Mars being so far away, this made such observations a little questionable. This is especially so, given the fact other astronomers didn't see the same thing at the time. Therefore, the few anomalies sighted could have been nothing more than a meteor impacting the planet, or a small asteroid.

To date, our Rovers on Mars have seen nothing of the sort in the way of such anomalies. So we must conclude there is little evidence for intelligent life on Mars, since we have nothing to support such a contention. There is virtually nothing to back such an idea.

This does not mean Mars didn't once have life. It may well have, although it is questionable whether the conditions on Mars ever allowed any such life to evolve to the level of intelligence. There doesn't seem to have been enough time for that. And evolution to intelligence took a long time on Earth, about three billion years!

So yes, intelligence life takes time and a lot of it. The dinosaurs had almost 200 million years to evolve, and as far as we know, they did not achieve any significant levels of intelligence. Mars faded early on. As mentioned, the planet seems to have been a failed experiment when it comes to life; at least for now (after all, we may live there someday, so it could support life again).

Getting back to our elimination process, this leaves our own Earth as a source for an alien species in our solar system, in which case they wouldn't really be aliens, just different from us. They'd be a different form of sentience, and an unknown species existing on our world (unknown to us).

Could a sentience species other than us have evolved on the Earth? Yes, of course, it could. We did, so why couldn't they? And they may have done this before we did. As possible examples, we have the dolphins. Many argue they are just as an intelligent species as we are, just in a different way, one foreign to "our way of thinking," so we have trouble recognizing this fact.

Then there are the cephalopods. This may surprise many, but cephalopods have been on Earth for a very long time. Moreover, they have been attributed with having high levels of intelligence. The octopus actually uses tools of a sort, responds "intelligently" when faced with some problem-solving tasks.

Squids, another cephalopod as well, are considered to be highly intelligent. Are they as intelligent as humans? We simply can't be sure. Again, their intelligence may be of such a different type we simply don't understand it well enough to be certain.

They also have an important drawback. The octopus and the squid are extremely short-lived compared to us. For the average squid, it would be just one to two years of life. For an octopus, it's about the same. Even giant squids may only average one to five years at most, although we know so little about those creatures, we can't be certain.

In any case, that's a very short time in which an individual member of their group can acquire knowledge and so evolve a complex and advanced technology. And as we know, the smaller versions of squids, and octopi, as well, are not the dominant species in our oceans, are not at the top of the food chain, as are we. Therefore, this would tend to show a lack of technology to give them this edge. This is assuming they even had any at all, which they probably don't.

And to back our argument further about intelligent aquatic species, neither of those species of cephalopods has developed any form of use of fire. Whether they are even capable of such seems unlikely. However, that the octopus, for instance, exhibits signs of intelligence, seems to be without question. In fact, we, the authors, are so convinced of this, we would no more eat calamari (squid) or octopus than we would eat a monkey's brains, as some cultures in the Far East do. The idea is simply anathema to us, personally.

We have no desire to kill and eat what may be fairly intelligent creatures, any more than we would have a desire to be cannibals. Sentient life should respect sentient life in our opinion, even if we are unsure of whether a species is intelligent or not. Better to err on the side of safety in such matters is our view. Eat something else is our motto.

So although, conceivably, the aliens could come from moons of either Saturn or Jupiter, we don't find those ideas very appealing, because of this whole question of their probably being aquatic in nature.

Perhaps this is just a bias on our part. Being human, we probably are anthropomorphizing the idea of where aliens should come from and what they should be like. Even so, we think it more likely a terrestrial form of intelligent species attaining the technology required so they are able to travel through space is more likely than an aquatic one would be.

Is it possible we are wrong in this? You bet! But we can only go by the Principle of Occam's Razor, and this leans toward a nonaquatic species achieving space flight more readily, more easily, and so more quickly than an aquatic one doing so.

In any case, we've eliminated the first two of the three alternatives. To recapitulate, these were:

1. The aliens are from our own solar system.

2. The aliens are from Earth, a different species from us. This leaves us with the third and final alternative as being most likely, which was:

3. The aliens are from elsewhere, and by elsewhere, we mean outside of our own solar system.

This then necessitates that they must have come here from one of the many millions, perhaps billions of Earthlike worlds out there in our galaxy or beyond. We think this is more likely a scenario than to think of them coming from the depths of an ocean on Europa or Callisto or other little moon with an ocean in our solar system.

This is not to say they couldn't be from there. There are those who argue they could well be. We don't rule them out for that reason. But again, we must go by the Principle of Occam's Razor, which leads us to our diaspora theory.

And before people shout at us that it is far more likely for an alien species in our own system to come to Earth than it is they come from elsewhere, we must remind them that even we now have the capabilities, albeit at tremendous cost and effort, of hollowing out asteroids and sending them off into deep space. So we know this is feasible for a fact. We don't know an aquatic species can ever conceive of technology such as we know it, or ever achieve such a thing in the crushing depths of the oceans of another alien world.

Chapter Conclusion. Therefore, our considered preference, based on everything stated above, would be our alien diaspora theory we've developed. That is, that any aliens on the Moon probably came from outside our solar system. For all we know, the Moon might well have, as well. Evidence seems to indicate it had some sort of very strange origins, and quite possibly not in the neighborhood of the Earth.

CHAPTER 21

What Are Aliens Doing On The Moon?

That the Moon now has a considerably thinner crust than was originally thought is a very recent discovery. Two gravity-mapping satellites, "Ebb" and "Flow," helped to determine this. The data from them was released late in 2012, after the two satellites ended their mission by being deliberately crashed into the Moon.

This, on the face of it, would give even more credence to the idea of a hollow Moon; because the data suggests the crust of the Moon is some 20 kilometers less in thickness than originally thought. Now scientists think the crust is only somewhere between 34 and 43 kilometers in total thickness, and the average thickness may be only on the order of about 30 kilometers. If true, then this lends even more credence to the idea the Moon may be hollow, having a considerably thinner shell or "outer hull" than was even first conjectured having.

What does this mean for the inhabitants of such a hollow Moon? Well, for one thing, it gives them more space in the interior. For another, if they were creating a camouflaged outer hull to hide the fact they were there; it would have taken considerably less effort to do so.

When one combines this with tales of strange "beacons of light" or "bands of light" streaking across the surface of that airless world, or "clouds," "vapors," "mists," and "smoke" appearing there (again, see NASA's own commissioned report on Transient Lunar Phenomena, Report R-277), it does make one wonder. Is someone taking surface excursions and/or venting waste gasses? But NASA itself said some of the things seen in its lunar photos may be from "outgassing."

Yes, many scientists say such a thing is highly unlikely, if not impossible, but do remember that in times past, they had similar rhetoric about the Moon with regard to certain things being "impossible."

Professor Bickerton, in 1926, categorically stated the very idea of sending something to the Moon was a notion that was not only "foolish," but flat out "impossible." He's not alone. A renowned astronomer, F. R. Moulton, in 1935 declared in writing, no less (always a mistake to record such absolutes on paper, probably), that humans would never be able to travel beyond our atmosphere and into outer space.

Mind you, this statement was made less than twenty-five years before satellites were successfully launched into space, so not only was he "categorically" wrong, but within just years he would be proven so.

It doesn't stop there. Professor Richard van der Riet Wooley in 1957, referred to the concept of any sort of space travel as "utter bilge." This former Astronomer Royal said this just a mere eight months before the Russians successfully launched their satellite, Sputnik I, into a close Earth orbit. How embarrassing for him!

Again, it doesn't pay to back one's self into a corner, not if one is a scientist and in the habit of declaring things impossible when they prove to be more than otherwise. The results of doing so are often then ending up as being made the butt of jokes and to be made to look ridiculous.

So the idea of "things being seen on the Moon" is not impossible, not hardly. Moreover, we have NASA's own commissioned report, one spanning centuries of data, to support such an idea as being true. Most scientists do think at least the majority of the observed events were real, and have tried, mostly unsuccessfully, to explain them in some way. Often the explanations seem more incredible than the events themselves.

In any case, "things" do seem to happen on the Moon, our supposedly dead-planet neighbor. Scientists seem at a loss as how to explain them. Oh, some are undoubtedly meteor impacts, but this would hardly account for "streaks," "flashes," "beacons," "pulsing glows," "bands of light," (meteors do not produce any sorts of streaks, flares, or glows on a world without atmosphere— only the impact could produce a flash or a flare of light). Nor does it account for all the other sorts of things seen.

There is one explanation that would account for all this. If there is a subterranean species of aliens upon the Moon, inhabiting its interior, then this would explain much. The flashes and glows could well be vehicles being launched from inside the Moon, or others landing there before being lowered below surface level. Mists and vapors in such cases could very well be expelled gases from the interior, just as we vent gases from time to time in various industrial operations.

Even the tracks and streaks upon the Moon are easily explained by the aliens occasionally choosing to take external excursions upon the surface of the Moon for whatever reasons (hull repair?). Maybe, they're just checking the outer hull of their space vessel? We're being a little flippant here again, but you get the idea.

Just about everything witnessed over the centuries would have one simple explanation, and that is aliens. If one were to apply the Principle of Occam's Razor here, that is the answer that would be the simplest and most all-encompassing.

So, just why are aliens on the Moon? Well, we think we've answered that, at least for the most part, and pretty well already. They live there. They dwell within the Moon. It's their home.

Why live so close to us? Well, the answer to that is a bit murkier. If indeed, the moon, Phobos of Mars, is hollow, and was once (or possibly could still be) a habitat of aliens, that would explain much. The aliens would have an interest, it seems, in planets that produce, or have produced life in the past. This would mean they are curious about other forms of life in general, and not necessarily specifically just with regard to us.

However, if Phobos is not a hollow moon, then again, things are a little harder to understand. It would mean the aliens parked the Moon near us for the specific purpose of being close to us, in particular.

And as you can see, we have just moved from the general (an interest in all life) to the specific (an interest in just us). This, at best, is a little disconcerting and not a little worrying. That sort of attention to such a degree tends to make us feel a little uncomfortable.

Nobody, and we mean nobody, would go to the trouble of moving a moon, or even hollowing out one that is already there, something the size of it, near a planet where there is life, unless they had some extraordinary interest in that particular life.

Remember, too, the aliens are most likely highly xenophobic. This means one would suppose they would not want to be close to any other species, and would prefer to keep their distance, perhaps dwell in the dark depths of interstellar space for as much time as possible. They would do this until refueling in the local solar systems, but then moving on, once more. After all, that would be the safest way, the best means of survival in a hostile universe.

So the aliens must have a compelling reason to be here, to stay here. Just what might that compelling reason be? In the next chapter we will try to undertake to answer that question in more detail.

What's more, we suspect that they have been here for quite some long time, indeed. There are a number of things we think likely. These are:

1. The aliens are here because of us and we've been here for a long time now, as well.

2. We think, judging by historical records and what has been ascertained about the Moon that it's been here at least at a minimum of thousands of years, and quite likely much longer, perhaps even millions. There are even those who think it might be billions of years.

3. The aliens must have some goal, plan, or need with regard to us, or they wouldn't expend so much time and energy, and take the risk of being this close to us, to overcome the xenophobia they almost assuredly have to some degree. This would not be a swift process.

4. The nature of this goal or plan is another one of those murky issues, but whatever it is, it seems to involve direct interference with us over the long term, given the available evidence.

With regard to this last point Number Four, there are some interesting ideas about this, not necessarily our own, of course, but which seem to have a real degree of possibility, if not even probability to them. There are those who think they are not only interfering with us, but are manipulating us to a large degree.

They base this assumption on (a) the numerous, one might even say, countless sightings of UFOs in our skies, and yes, even in our seas and lakes (sometimes even rivers), as well, and (b) on the fact of alien abductions, which they believe may number in the millions, and certainly in the hundreds of thousands.

They point to the theory of ancient aliens and various items of evidence indicating these extraterrestrial intelligences might have been here for a very long time. Moreover, there are those who think the alien interference is being aided and abetted by our own governments, and there is a conspiracy or plot to keep their presence as secret as possible. Furthermore, there are those who think the reason for this secrecy is some form of grand experiment is being performed, and open knowledge of it would affect the results.

There are others who say the reason for the secrecy is the aliens are either in control or assuming control, and "those in the know" have decided to play along for whatever personal reasons they may have, perhaps their own survival in the long term. Shades of the *X-Files!*

As to these last points, we simply can't be sure how close to the truth or not they may be. But the fact the aliens have a compelling reason to be here would seem obvious. Again no one moves worlds around, or hollows them out just for the heck of it. And those that can survive better on their own, well away from others, possibly hostile or at least potentially hostile species, are sacrificing much in the way of their safety in order to be this close to another alien species, meaning us.

Please understand, by using the word "sacrificing," we don't necessarily mean in the good sense, as in sacrificing one's self for another. They may be sacrificing their safety and comfort levels just in order to achieve something that is worth the effort, the risk, and so worth that particular sacrifice. Whatever that goal is, it would seem to involve us in many ways, one might even say to an intimate level.

Here's an interesting point; the aliens' technology must be far advanced beyond our own. Whatever it is they wanted, they could now, or at least in times past, have probably exacted it from us by brute force and probably with relative ease into the bargain, if it was possible to do so. Again, if it would be so easy today, with our burgeoning planet-wide population, it might've been very easy in the past, when our species numbered much less. This, they may have done. We just can't be sure. Some say they did.

Therefore, whatever the aliens want or need from us, it for some reason must involve a degree of subtlety (and we use the word "degree" advisedly here), to want to maintain the relative secret of their existence. We use the term "relative" because remember, over a million UFO sightings, on average occur each year around the Earth. So this secrecy could be either with various governments' collusion in the cover-up, or not.

The only possible alternative to this idea is the aliens don't think they're being secretive at all. Perhaps by their standards, they are not. Maybe, the way they're behaving is considered open by their values, being a naturally secretive and withdrawn people, perhaps by our standards only.

After all, having evolved into a xenophobic and secretive species by nature, maybe this is as open as "they" get. Maybe, this is their norm. In other words, what appears to us, being a much more open people, to be a conspiracy of secrecy surrounding them, from their perspective may not be at all. "They" might think they're doing all this in the plain light of day.

After all, they fly through our skies with seeming impunity by day and by night. Numerous photos and videos have been taken of such events. Thousands upon thousands claim to have been abducted by them. There are even those who claim there are wrecked alien spaceships being held in secret places by our governments.

So it's not exactly as if the aliens are trying very hard to hide their presence. Therefore, any secrecy or conspiracy may be attached strictly to the whole affair by our own governments' attempts to avoid the public being upset or panicked by the existence of such creatures. This could well be.

There does seem to have been an overt attempt to cause ridicule for anyone who even reports UFO sightings, especially with regard to those who are trained in observation, such as airline pilots (both military and commercial) and others, as well. The result is often the destruction of their career, or demotions, and often even forced retirements. At the very least, they're made to look absurd.

As just one example, a Japanese commercial airline pilot spotted a UFO while flying over Alaska. He radioed this in. The sighting was corroborated by another commercial jet plane in the area. Radar even tracked it.

Yet, ultimately, he was reassigned to a "desk job" shortly after the event, which means in other words, his career as a pilot was over for good. This is not uncommon in these cases. In America, pilots who claim to have seen UFOs often are made to take mandatory psychological tests, to consult a psychiatrist. This goes on their official records. The stigma of this prevents many of them from formally reporting such events.

Chapter Conclusion. So is there a conspiracy of silence? It could well be, but this might be for a good reason. Our governments, as many conspiracy theorists point out, may just be trying to protect us from ourselves, to keep us from panicking.

Would we? If we knew, would we panic? That's a matter for conjecture and would depend on the circumstance of just what the aliens are doing here. Undoubtedly, there would be some who would. Undoubtedly, there would also be many who would not.

In any case, just how successful our governments have been in this regard, maintaining the existence of UFOs as a secret, when the majority of Americans now think UFOs exist, is a moot point. It is now one open for considerable debate. A more cynical viewpoint of all this might be the government isn't so concerned about our safety, and that's why they're keeping the secret, but they are afraid they would be toppled from power, and have a new government replace them if the truth were known.

It's a common thing for governments to fall and people no longer to have faith in them. It's even a common thing for new types of governments to replace such. Those with position, wealth, and the power that comes with it, might be very partial to keeping things just the way they are. They have the largest stake in the status quo.

Those who "have it all," are the most resistant to change, because any such change could take what they have away from them. To be blunt here, and again rather cynical, such people would have every reason to want things to seem, at least, to stay just the way they are. They would want this for as long as it was possible to make it so.

The long dark night may be coming, but just not during their lifetime, is probably the attitude such people might have. Of course this is mere supposition on our part, but it is based on the more basic aspects of human nature. We're referring specifically to those who need power, and are greedy for it, crave it. It's only "natural" that once they have it, they don't want to let go.

Would you? Would you want to give up your mansion, your billions, your fleet of automobiles, your yacht, your jetting about the planet, furs and jewelry, to let people know that "they are out there?" Personally, we could imagine ourselves wanting to wait quite a while for that to happen, if we were that wealthy. After all, we'd want time to enjoy our wealth, too! And just as they probably do.

Or just maybe, the long dark night is falling and they are powerless to stop it, to do anything about it. Their silence might be out of their shame, their inability to do anything to save us. Our government may be powerless in the face of the aliens' vastly superior power. Perhaps they are just trying to hold things together for as long as they can.

CHAPTER 22

The Compelling Reason For Aliens To Come Here?

Why have aliens come here? Well, we've mentioned one reason already. The Earth is abundant with life in general. Maybe our planet just makes for a fascinating study of alien life forms (alien to them, at least). This could well be. After all, the Earth swarms with different forms of life.

However, we think there is another reason, a more likely one. Yes, the aliens are interested in life and no doubt in a general sense, but also in a much more specific sense, as well. We think there compelling reason for being here is us. By us, we mean humans. We are convinced of this.

We are probably the focus of their attention. If we were not, if it was just the resources of the Planet Earth, they could easily have swept us aside and just taken what they wanted. So by logical deduction, it is us they are interested in.

Having the Moon so close to Earth, their habitat, which also acts as a base, is just an incredible convenience for them. It is a safe place to sally forth from, being far enough away from us, where our technology really is of no serious threat to them. Yet they are close enough for them to come to Earth whenever they like. Considering the level of their technology, such should be a speedy and easy feat to accomplish whenever they want.

To put it another way, they are like children who consider themselves safe in the upper limbs of the tree, and shouting epitaphs and making faces at those walking below. They can do what they like with impunity, because no one is going to be able to get to them, not having either the prowess or the urge to risk climbing so high to confront them. Sadly, they are most certainly not like children when it comes to being innocent, without guile, or purpose. They are our superiors.

Make no mistake. This is what the aliens have in the way of a relationship to us. They occupy the "High Ground." And as any military strategist will tell you, he who has the high ground, has the distinct advantage in any sort of military action. Add to that a superior technology, and the apparent ability to dominate our skies, and it would appear that we are mostly powerless against them.

Perhaps the buzzing of our military vehicles, military bases, and our commercial aircraft are just a not-so-gentle reminder of their capability. By suddenly turning off our nuclear missiles launch readiness, maybe they are demonstrating just how powerful they are. And yes, they actually did this at one military base. Please go to: http://www.cufon.org/cufon/malmstrom/malm1.htm for an account of this. We can't seem to account for such activity otherwise.

If our governments are aware of an alien existence, and we think they certainly are, perhaps they just can't divulge it, because they were told not to in no uncertain terms. And to defy such a demand, could mean devastating results. We doubt our governments would have the power to stop such results, such possible consequences, in any case.

Again the aliens control the high ground. And for all our military jets and nukes, notwithstanding, they most likely control the skies closer to ground, as well. Again, the aliens rule the sky.

It's not a pleasant thought, we know. And sometimes it is hard for people to understand just what the consequences of such a statement really are. Please understand; this means the aliens can do what they want, what they will with us, if they so choose and they may be doing just that! This is our predicament as humans, as unlikely as it may seem.

Still, it would seem to be the situation. It's simple logic. If aliens exist, if they have the apparent UFO capabilities that so many people have cited, then they have a superior technology to us. Judging by the descriptions of their vessels, they would appear to be vastly superior. If this is so, then our aircraft are no match for them. Again, this means they rule the skies. It's that straightforward and no matter how one looks at it, the answer comes out the same. Why do we repeat this? Well, it's because although we may intellectually understand this… to some degree, the average human probably doesn't get the full implications. We see lights in the sky that can do things nothing else can do. We see strange craft zipping overhead. But the consequences of this, very real consequences seem to escape us. We may well be powerless in every sense of the word, in every way against "them."

Yet, we live with it. Remember, many people think aliens do exist. Again, just over half, the majority of Americans think UFOs are real. If this is the case, then the only conclusion we can come to, is that somewhere, on some level, people know the aliens are superior to us in their technology, and therefore, we would have little hope in any sort of fight with them. Yet, we go on with our lives despite this fact. Humanity, it seems, is marvelously resilient in its capacity to deal with the incredible.

Still, if this is true, if aliens exist and have this power over us, what does this really mean for us humans? Well for whatever compelling reason(s) the aliens are here; one thing should be eminently clear to all of us and that is we are not, as we have long thought we were, at the top of the food chain. There is something above even us, for better or worse.

If the abductions are real, for example, and we think they are, then we are being taken like so many cattle for purposes unknown, and returned slightly less than in original condition, at the very least, according to those interviewed.

The argument seems to be not whether all of this is happening, but whether the aliens' intentions are for the ultimate good, or are more inimical, hostile in nature. As we mentioned in our other book, ***The Darker Side Of The Moon "They" Are Watching Us!*** the reasons for the aliens' actions are perhaps not the most important thing for us humans. It is the results of those actions that are of concern to us. Since we can't do anything about what "they" are doing, we can only hope it doesn't destroy us as a species in the process, or at least if it does, it is to replace us with a better version, perhaps? But the question then is; whose idea of "better—ours or theirs? And guess what the answer to that is. Yes, it doesn't take a great leap of imagination here to arrive at that, unfortunately.

One thing is certain; whatever the aliens are doing to us, for good or ill, it is a violation of our basic human rights as we see them, for them to abduct us with us having no say in the matter. If they are exploring human nature by experimenting on us and it is without our permission that is also a violation of our basic human rights.

If aliens are doing this for some greater good, a good of which we are not aware, it still doesn't matter to us as individuals. If you are jailed for the rest of your life, even though you're innocent, it doesn't matter to you society did it for the best possible reasons, the highest motivations, because you're the one who's going to suffer the penalty.

And the "program" they have may be subtle, long term. So we do think we should watch out for be some signs that what is happening may not be to our benefit, just in case. Just as an example of the type of thing we're talking about, researchers have become aware that the sperm count in men is the western world is dropping. Overall, it is down from 100 million viable sperm cells per milliliter to just 60 million on the average. This is, of course, a

40 percent drop. Worse, some results say 15 and 20 percent of males, (male youths) show a sperm count of just 20 million. This is defined, technically, to be in the abnormal (abnormally low) range.

Furthermore, although this was thought to possibly result from environmental influences on men (such as the wearing of tight underwear, etc.), this has not been found to be the case. Instead, many researchers now think this negative change occurs sometime during gestation, when the male child is still in the womb. The question of course, then, is why? What's suddenly going on that wasn't going on before? We just don't know the answer to that yet, and it is the not knowing that is of concern here.

And remember, we do have quite a number of rather alarming claims about women who are abducted and then artificially inseminated by their alien abductors. If true, is there a correlation between this and the precipitous drop in the western male's sperm counts?

That's not all. Over the last thirty years, we've seen an alarming, truly alarming rise in the rate of children (mostly males, but females, as well) being born who then suffer from autism. Once considered a relative rarity in the 1960's and 1970's, autism is now at "epidemic proportions" as many researchers have declared it.

The percentage of children with autism has continued to rise. The rate reached as high as one in every one hundred children born in just the last couple of decades. This was unprecedented and alarmed researchers. Worse was to come. Just very recently, the Center for Disease Control says the figure has now gone up to one in every sixty-eight children having autism! The problem is growing, and growing fast! It's rapidly approaching the point where this could become of truly major significance for society, having a constantly and rapidly growing population of children who require extensive medical care throughout their lives, many of whom simply can't function well without constant support/care.

Are we saying aliens may be behind this with their supposedly numerous (millions some claim) abductions of people? No, we're not, but it would be foolish not to consider such things, just in case. You see, we have no idea why there are so many abductions, to such an incredible extent. But if they are happening, and we suspect they are, then it has to be for some purpose, for some "program" on a large scale being conducted by the aliens.

So not to watch what's happening to us and our lives, our children, and our world would be foolish. We can't just assume these countless abductions are just for "harmless' experiments upon us. Just to be on the safe side, we have to assume something worse just might be going on, as well.

Now, let us make it clear here we don't want to sound like alarmists in any way. We aren't over-the-top conspiracy theorists. And truthfully, we'll say right up front we have absolutely no idea whatsoever why autism is reaching ever worse levels, is becoming an ongoing and increasing epidemic with all that such may portend for society. Nor do we know why the male sperm count is dropping so precipitously. These were just meant as examples only, of possible things we should look out for and also consider. Again, the changes the aliens may (or may not) be introducing may be subtle, long term, and so easy to miss… until too late, perhaps?

But let us declare here, the reason for these particular medical conditions is best left to professional medical researchers to figure out. This we freely and gladly admit. And we make no claims as to the cause of these things at all. Again, these were just examples to illustrate a point; that point is: we don't know why aliens are supposedly abducting over a million people, why they are "probing" and performing strange medical procedures on them.

And it is the not knowing that concerns us. What are the long-term results of such interference? What are the consequences? Since we just don't know, we should be wary, pay attention, and look for answers to these questions. This is all we're saying here.

After all, if the aliens are friends to us, we have no problems. But if they are not, if their intentions are the opposite, we should keep in mind their tactics may not be to conquer us outright, but perhaps to use more subtle methods to reduce our population numbers, and/or our ability as a species to continue to exist. We simply can't overlook any possibilities, not when our future as humans is at stake. Everything, however outlandish it may seem, should at least be considered, just to be safe. We need to be "on the lookout." It's that simple.

When something strange seems to be happening, maybe, just maybe we should check it out. But no, we definitely aren't saying autism and/or low sperm counts are the result of alien interference. Of course, we aren't saying they aren't, either. We simply don't know.

Chapter Conclusion. So to summarize this chapter, yes we think aliens are here. We think they inhabit the Moon. Whether this is the entire interior of the Moon, or just huge caverns—does it really matter? If they are there, if they do rule our skies, as we think they do, and are doing even a portion of what people say they are doing to humans, then it would appear they have a compelling reason to be here.

One more time, that reason is "us." Their motive for being here is the existence of humanity on this planet. Whether they created us, are manipulating us, just interfering with us, and/or just performing experiments on us, doesn't matter.

If the Moon is hollow and aliens rule the sky, this is because they are primarily interested in us. This is their compelling reason for being here. And if so, then we have an equally compelling interest to want to know why and just what they may be up to, and if it is for our good or ill.

CHAPTER 23
Xenophobia And Hostility

We've already shown how the aliens could well suffer from a probable xenophobia, a major social/racial form of that condition. We've also mentioned how even any non-hostile race would acquire this in all probability. This would be as a natural form of a survival mechanism in a universe that could very well be patently a hostile environment, a very unsafe place in which to exist. Those who shun other races are less likely to encounter hostile ones, ones who might destroy them, commit genocide upon them. It is simply a good idea to have some form of xenophobia for this reason, at least to some degree. Perhaps we should have it a bit more?

So by logical progression, those races who would survive over the long haul, and we're talking millions, possibly even billions of years here, would tend to be the most xenophobic ones of all. This would be a process not very different from natural selection in evolution. Some could well argue it is the same thing as evolution. Xenophobia would be a beneficial trait for any intelligent species to select for as a strong survival attribute.

What we haven't gone into here yet is what the hostile races would be like. They, too, would be xenophobic for much the same reason. Perhaps even more so, for not only would they be afraid of competitive races that might be out to actively destroy them, but they might just have the ill-will of any survivors of a species they've already attacked, but somehow didn't manage to completely wipe out.

Author Greg Bear uses this very premise for his plot in his much hailed science fiction book, The Forge Of God. But we're not talking science fiction here. We're talking about a very possible, perhaps even probable scenario.

Moreover, if aliens naturally develop into a species that has diasporas, and this would seem likely, especially if faster-than-light travel simply isn't in the cards (as most scientists think), this would then be a probability. Some portions of a species, hidden in habitats inside of asteroids, moonlets, and moons, would be far more likely to escape the hostile race's notice.

They could slip off into the eternal night of interstellar space, evade detection, as it were, and so survive for long periods of time in such a way. And some, if survivors of prior attacks by more hostile species, might well decide they want revenge, or at the very least, to remove such a major threat to their continued existence. Furthermore, a long-lived species could wait for millennia or even longer, if necessary, to wreak such revenge or threat removal upon their enemies.

This threat of retaliation would add to any hostile race's xenophobia. They would not just have a generalized fear of other intelligent species with which they might have to worry about competing with in general, but they would have the nagging fear of reprisals by those possible survivors of races they've already attacked.

This means xenophobia would be a trait selected for in both the hostile and non-hostile species of intelligent life alike, but may manifest itself even more so in the hostile ones. Does this sound like a contradiction?

Well, it isn't. Xenophobia, in its most extreme forms can, and has even here on Earth, led to genocide. To wipe out something you don't understand, something that seems different and foreign, something you may then fear, and fear greatly, is a very common thing among humans. If other intelligences are similar to us in any way at all, they may develop the same characteristics in that regard, as well, at least in some variation of it or other.

This means a secretive and hidden intelligent species could also be bent on the destruction of other intelligent species they might see as a threat, whether the threat is real or not. It's a matter of how they would view the matter through "xenophobic eyes," as it were.

This would color all their perceptions. As in example, just as in the 1950's (and even now to some degree), monster movies show how we viewed the idea of anything "alien," and "not of this Earth" as one movie title went, as being horrible and something to be feared, real aliens just might feel the same way, and with real reason!

Now for the big question; does this attitude of intense hostility toward others apply to aliens who may live and dwell below the Moon's surface? Well, we have to say it is a distinct possibility that it does. The possibility does exist.

However, the good news is if they were bent on our genocide, logic would seem to dictate they would have already accomplished this and Earth would no longer bear human life today.

Since the Earth still does have us living on it, our hollow-Moon aliens must not want this fate for us, our demise, and so must not have xenophobia to such an overwhelming degree. Or if they still might, then perhaps some other motivation, an even greater one exists for keeping us around when they really might want us obliterated. That is, of course, unless they are slowly reducing our numbers over the long term and we just aren't aware of this fact yet, because the results haven't yet manifested themselves to us.

But if they do want to keep us around, just what might such a motivation be? Well, it could be any number of things. However, the most likely is they need us. For some reason and despite their xenophobia, they have to keep us around because they need us for some purpose. This could be because:

1. They need help in obtaining resources, and if not now, perhaps they did in our far past, as many Ancient Aliens theorists believe might have been the case (using us to mine minerals, etc.).

2. We act as a camouflage, a diversion. What better way to hide from your enemies than by being close by another target, one loudly screaming its existence through the continued broadcast of radio waves?

Any hostiles would see us as the target and so might not even notice the existence of another and hidden species close by. In other words, we could be an excellent distraction, merrily beaming our existence via radio and television out into the galaxy, while they remain in seclusion and secret safety very close by.

3. We might be a means or resource in and of ourselves. Many UFO and Ancient Alien theorists believe we actually are being harvested, or used as incubators for their own offspring. They base this idea on the numerous abductions claimed, and/or the animal mutilations where specific organs of animals are removed cleanly and with "surgical precision." Yes, people really do believe this and cite a good deal of evidence to support their conclusions.

4. Or, the case might also be they feel the need of an ally, a species with a large population they can utilize in time of great need, if necessary. With their technology, their apparent ability to control us if they choose to do so, we might be nothing more than a vast army of drones-in-waiting should they need to mobilize against another powerful hostile race. Perhaps, they think (maybe with real reason) that we can be easily manipulated to their ends, as in "we must help our Space Brothers."

5. Alternatively, maybe we're being groomed as potential allies. They could see us as a young species with potential, as possible future allies. One way to protect one's self from other hostile species might well be to form alliances with other friendly species. The "safety in numbers" idea might well be their goal. Let's hope so.

6. More darkly, we may be the subject of some vast experiment on their part, to have as a "sample" race of intelligent beings to learn from, so they can better study how to defend themselves from other sentient species that unlike us are a real threat. Or they may have some other goal in mind in this regard, one we simply can't yet fathom.

Chapter Conclusion. There could well be other reasons, ones we haven't thought of, but then not having the mind of an alien, maybe there is some other motivation for keeping us around when they would prefer us dead we just can't think of. It's very possible we just don't have the turn of mind, or the type of mind they do, to think of such alternatives.

So are there alternatives to some of these grim premises? Of course, and we'll look at these in the next chapter.

CHAPTER 24
Maybe Xenophobic, But Still Our Alien Friends?

We've just stated some of the worst case scenarios in the prior chapter. However, perhaps just the opposite is true. It could also be despite an ingrained and ages-old cultivated xenophobia for survival reasons that the aliens see us as no threat and have no wish to harm us. Perhaps, it's just an extreme shyness, a reclusive attitude on their part keeping them from interacting more openly with us?

After all, when you've been afraid of anything "foreign" for thousands and possibly millions of years, such entrenched habits may simply be impossible to overcome completely. They would certainly have an effect on their behavior. This would be so, even if they wanted to be friendly.

Do we think this is the likely case? No, unfortunately, we do not. There has simply been too much evidence of UFOs openly endangering our lives on occasion. As mentioned, there is the "buzzing" of our military bases, commercial airliners and private planes in broad daylight and often at great peril to the lives of the passengers and crew of those craft.

There have even been cases of deaths connected to UFO sightings, as with the young civilian pilot in Australia. Please go to:

http://ufologie.patrickgross.org/htm/valentich.htm   for more on this. Then there is the case of the nine students in Russia in the late 1950s at the Dyatlov Pass Incident, as it is called now. Please go to:

http://www.forteantimes.com/features/articles/1562/the_dyatlov_pass_incident.html.

Or another incident was the case of the Russian navy submarine divers who also died while involved in a USO (Unidentified Submerged Object) occurrence. Please go to:

http://rt.com/news/russian-navy-ufo-records-say-aliens-love-oceans/ to see more on this, as well.

They are not alone. There have been others, as well as those who have been injured in numerous ways, or had their lives ruined or disrupted. Again, deaths have resulted and far more of them than you might think!

If you'd like to read more on this (and this includes deaths of UFO investigators, as well), Close Encounters of the Fatal Kind by Nick Redfern, is a new book due out this summer (2014). So if we are "alarmist" about this subject, we aren't alone in thinking this.

So just shyness doesn't seem to be entirely the case here. On the contrary, it would appear the aliens have an almost arrogant disregard for our personal safety and us, as well as a fundamental disdain for our concept of human rights, and even our liberty, as in the case of abductions. At the very least, this smacks of an almost smug sense of superiority that is racially or technologically based, perhaps. Possibly, it is both. There almost seems to be, by the numerous demonstrations of their past behavior toward us in these UFO instances, a complete contempt and/or condescending attitude toward us humans as a species, and as individuals.

If this is the case, if they are so "superior minded," this could well be another reason why we still exist. Despite a powerful xenophobia toward us, they may simply feel assured we are no threat whatsoever toward them. They can use and abuse us any way they like without fear of repercussions.

Who knows? We might also even be a source of amusement for them. When a child burns ants with a magnifying glass, does he stop to worry about what the ant may think, about how it might feel about its life being taken and destroyed for someone's mere casual amusement? Do researchers give any real concern to how mice in a laboratory experiment might feel? Maybe, that's just the way the aliens see us, in just that same sort of inferior way.

Alternatively, they could be trying to help us. Since we're still here, it could be they are not a hostile race, and are actually hiding close by to act as guardians to us. After all, being as babies to them, and just now beginning to kick and scream in our cradles (and beaming those "baby" noises out to the galaxy without thinking of the consequences), maybe they are here to watch over us. It may be they feel a duty to protect us until we "come of age," and can fend for ourselves in a galaxy of fierce competition, one of a hostile nature.

This is a possibility and a reasonable one to consider, as well. After all, we humans have evolved compassion and empathy for others, so why not alien races evolving the same way? This might even be a probability, because after all, alliances, forging friendly ties with other species, might be a very good way to counteract the danger of hostile species. A sense of compassion and empathy might just make for a very good survival trait, evolutionary-wise.

Of course, this is not a new concept. Even the old original ***Star Trek*** television series had the idea of a friendly and compassionate "Federation of Planets" opposing "evil empires." However, that concept was based on how we saw ourselves in the United States, as opposed to the Soviet Union of the Cold War era. In other words, the original ***Star Trek*** series was a reflection of our bitter relations with Russia at the time, of the then-current political events.

Even so, the idea of helpful aliens still has merit. The axiom, "there is safety in numbers," must hold on the galactic and universal scale, just as it does on the earthly scale. The idea of aliens helping other species in order to better their own chances of survival has considerable appeal as a survival strategy for all concerned. After all, there is always more than one evolutionary strategy for survival.

Of course, one then has to ask why hide from us? Why, if they exist at all, live secretly within the Moon, conceal their existence from us? Again, there may be many reasons for this. Some of the main ones are:

1. They do not wish to cause us undue fear.

2. Perhaps they fear us. We are great in numbers, after all and if they have a strong case of xenophobia, such a fear would be natural.

3. They do not wish to destroy our culture by revealing a vastly superior one exists close by, as with Europe destroying the cultures of the Americas they discovered and then interacted with, to the terrible detriment of those native cultures, and always without exception causing, even inadvertently at times, grave damage to them.

4. Perhaps we are just not socially or technologically "ready" to meet them face on and in an open situation. Again, to refer to *Star Trek*, the Federation did not contact species until it felt they were ready to be so contacted, had reached a certain stage in their development when they were prepared. Development of a warp drive was the usual measuring stick the Federation used for this purpose.

Well, maybe we haven't yet developed such a thing (and such a thing may be impossible under the laws of physics, in any case), or reached some similar alien idea of readiness to be contacted by them yet.

5. Another alternative might be that they do not wish to interfere with this, but would rather we develop in our own way, with perhaps just guidance from them, but in a subtle fashion.

Perhaps they are sort of alien tutors, galactic guidance counselors, if you will.

6. Possibly, as mentioned earlier, we are the subject of a vast experiment, but one that is for our benefit. Maybe they are gently, but persistently trying to develop a new species out of this, a superior one, and one that is better able to meet the challenges of an uncaring universe.

To put it in plain English, perhaps if we were dogs instead of humans, we are more like lovable cocker spaniels, when in order to survive long term we need to be more like pit bulls. So it could be the aliens are doing what they must to help ensure our survival as a species, even if it is rather unpleasant for some of us as individuals.

The only problem with any of these scenarios is again, their behavior towards many of our aircraft, military bases, and individual members of society. This still presents a problem with any of these options. Why would a basically beneficent people behave in such a summary way toward us, if they intended us no harm?

Well, the answer to that could be very simple. Maybe, we humans need to stop thinking about aliens as we do, just in black and white. After all, they are living creatures, too. No matter how advanced they might be, or how evolved, they probably still are capable of making mistakes on the individual level, as well as the group level.

Maybe, the problem lies with us. Maybe, we, as a species, need to grow up and stop thinking of possible aliens as either angels or demons, our deadly enemies, or "our space brothers" or even as "space enemies."

In all likelihood, they are probably neither, but something between those two extremes. They are almost assuredly not a monolithic species, being just so many robots that all think and behave exactly alike. We don't, so why should they? There must be a range, a spectrum of behavior patterns on their part, depending upon the individual aliens involved, and just as there is with us humans.

If this is so, then this would explain some of the more aberrant-seeming behavior on their part. Then again, they might've had other very valid reasons for doing what they did. In some cases, their own craft might've been in danger and there was no way out other than to cause damage to our own aircraft in the process of escaping us. In the case of the military bases, perhaps those were warnings they wouldn't countenance us actually firing our nuclear weapons in a war, showing us they could interfere to stop us from annihilating ourselves.

Alternatively, perhaps they had some overwhelming need to behave the way they did, and we just don't understand it from our perspective. Does a bird understand why we take it to the veterinarian if it has a damaged wing? It can't comprehend why we are doing such a thing, but we have an ulterior motive, to try to make it better. Still, during the process, the bird doesn't know this, nor may it ever understand, even though ultimately it can fly once more.

So perhaps this sort of thing is true of the aliens. Maybe, they are just doing what's best for us, whether we like it or not? We may not comprehend or appreciate this, but then most children don't understand the concept of a parent's tough love, either. Perhaps that's how the aliens see us, as mere children on the galactic scene and requiring some of that "tough love."

So we can't say for sure if the aliens are hostiles, or just very xenophobic friends. However, so numerous have some of the UFO incidents been, and so many seem to be the cases of abductions, that we authors feel there is more to their motivations than just a simple case of them using tough love on us. If it is a form of tough love, it's akin to a doctor using a medicine that sometimes kills, perhaps almost as often as it cures. Then again, maybe we need this and don't realize it. Who knows what pressing concerns they may have for our future?

Chapter Conclusion. We don't know about you, but we would expect more from an advanced species. Even as we find alternative ways of doing things better, we would expect they might, as well. So far, we've seen little of this in evidence on their part. Then, perhaps this is just our limited perspective on the issue and we simply don't have all the facts. Of course, we probably don't and perhaps that would explain much.

Now, having discussed what the aliens might be like in a hollow Moon, one has to wonder exactly how long they might've been here. Well we've already broached the subject to some degree, but we would like to take the topic a little further. This we will do in our next chapter.

CHAPTER 25

How Long Have "They" Really Been Here?

If the Moon is hollow, or at least possessing large hollow spaces within it, and aliens are there, then just how long might they have been there? Well, we've already discussed some of the available evidence and it strongly hints the Moon might not always have been in this neck of the woods.

We've also mentioned the theory of Ancient Aliens a number of times now. But let's delve into this aspect of things just a bit more, see what evidence we can find for these ideas, as to whether the Moon has been here for a very long time, millions or even billions of years, or just thousands.

Enormous time spans. The first thing we have to understand in all of this is the aliens, based on the scenarios (any of them given here in this book), must think in the long term. And by the long term, we mean very long term, indeed.

Any race who can span the star systems, especially if doing so at less than the speed of light, are thinking in terms of millions, if not billions of years. In fact, they may be intent on surviving for the life of the universe, or ultimately, even beyond it, if that's in some way possible.

Does this idea seem incredible? It shouldn't. Already, we humans are thinking along these lines ourselves. Science show after science show, on the Discovery Channel, Science Channel, History Channel, and others, talk about the various projected lifespans of humanity, how it will all end, and how humanity might somehow survive even that ending.

If we, at our relatively primitive stage of existence are already contemplating this, why shouldn't more advanced species, ones who have already attained the stars, not do the same? It's just a matter of logic. And logic, at least, must be the same everywhere in the universe, or it wouldn't work here. So why wouldn't alien races be looking for exit strategies from a dying universe, as well, or at least for long-term survival strategies within this universe? Of course, they would.

Therefore, where we might think a human generation or even a century is a long time and so a very long time to plan for, that would be as nothing compared to how an alien species traveling the depths of interstellar space would probably view things. To undertake the probable diasporas we've already mentioned here, would be to undertake something they didn't just spend one or two generations on, or even several. No, it would be thousands if not tens of thousands, or even more.

Even to travel to their nearest neighboring star system would take thousands of years at sub-light speeds. This is why their asteroid or moon habitats would have to be self-sustaining, and totally self-contained, if perhaps, with unoccupied asteroids and comets as a form of resupply (baggage train) tagging along with them.

Why do we seem to "harp" on this long-term strategy? Well, because we think this is a pivotal part of any species' makeup that travels to the stars, that it must form an integral part of their alien psyche. If this wasn't so at the outset of their journeys, such a strong character trait, such a viewpoint/perspective would almost certainly have to develop along the way.

If they wanted to survive, long-term strategizing would come with time for them as a matter of course, we feel, because not only do we (and they) shape our surroundings, but our surroundings then shape us, as well. Our surroundings mold us, form us over time. The same would be true of any aliens.

As we stated earlier, even we have the capability, albeit at a great expense and effort, of launching a hollowed-out asteroid into the depths of interstellar space. We, too, could cause other asteroids, and perhaps even comets to be shepherded along with such a habitat for resupply sources during such an interminable journey. However, we would be limited to a sub-light speed.

Although the aliens, being far more advanced than we are, might be capable of faster-than-light speeds, again, many of our physicists think this just might be impossible. Even so, there have been some tantalizing bits of evidence, some of the faintest clues lately, saying it just might be conceivable under the right circumstances. Still as of this writing, there is nothing even close to definite with regard to the idea that faster-then-light travel can or does exist.

So for practical purposes, once more, we are basing the ideas in this book on the fact of the aliens being restricted by the same laws of physics as we currently are, or at least know them to be. This can change, of course, and we freely admit this fact. However, if some alien species can travel faster than the speed of light, then even so, time could still well be a huge factor for them in any case.

Who knows how much faster than the speed of light they could then travel? Even our nearest neighbor, the star, Alpha Centauri (a triple-star system, actually), is almost 4-½ light years away from us. This means that traveling even at the speed of light would take us 4-½ years to get there. For star systems that are hundreds or thousands of light years away from us, this means that even at the speed of light, it would take (obviously) hundreds or thousands of years to get to those.

So even if the aliens had faster-then-light (FTL) capabilities, they might still have to think in the very long term. This is simply because their FTL abilities may have limitations as to how fast they can go, and the energy consumption such an effort would require. This is another reason we support the idea of them developing long-term thinking as a matter of course. Again, it is just for eminently practical reasons they would do so.

Furthermore, our concept of how the aliens might spread throughout the galaxy and even beyond requires no feats of magic, pseudo-science, or belief in that which we have not yet accomplished or invented for ourselves, such as the ability to travel faster than the speed of light. We aren't saying this won't someday be possible. In fact, we rather suspect it just might be. But again, for our purposes, we choose the simplest explanation according to the Principle of Occam's Razor.

Either way, aliens probably do think in the long-term and at least some of them have been traveling to the stars for a very long time, indeed, perhaps millions, if not billions of years. To reiterate, this means they could have arrived here hundreds, thousands, tens of thousands, millions, or possibly even billions of years ago. And they or others like them may have come several times over. More than one species may have visited here.

Remember, the theory of an intelligent species' expansion states that even at reasonably normal speeds, those far less than that of light, the galaxy can be completely colonized in a few tens of millions of years. Given the age of the universe, this means this could already have been accomplished and repeatedly by different alien species.

Evidence we've compiled and shown earlier in this book seems to indicate they may have arrived sometime around 10,000 to 15,000 years ago, Yet, there is other evidence to say they may have been here much longer. Which version of these two possibilities do we go with? Well, the truth is, there seems to be about the same amount of evidence for both.

The idea of a shorter term for the Moon being here. Here are some reasons why we find the idea of the Moon only having been here a relatively short while to have equal support, as the idea of the Moon having been here for a very long time:

1. Historical evidence, written and oral, as well as in the form of legends from various cultures worldwide say the Moon hasn't always been in our skies, that it just "appeared" there in the early days of human civilization. Although the dates vary, they do seem to fall within the 10,000-to-15,000-year range, again, give or take a couple thousand years.

2. We find it a strange coincidence that during this very period, human civilization suddenly started, "as if overnight," as some archaeologists and historians have phrased it, and then flourished. There is no doubt that for thousands upon thousands of years we existed as a species on this world, but it was only during that particular period we "suddenly" developed civilization.

Again, some archaeologists refer to it as having been "an explosion," and one "worldwide," not just restricted to one region of the planet, as would have seemed likely at first. After all, logic would seem to dictate someone would discover the basics of civilization somewhere. Then the information would slowly disseminate from there, gradually and slowly spreading around the planet. This is not the case. The "explosion" of civilization seemed to take place in multiple regions simultaneously.

3. And why just then did it happen and not thousands of years before or after? We have no record of humans slowly developing "upward" in their skills toward any sort of a takeoff point for civilization. Our ancestors used pretty much the same primitive methods for countless generations. They were, in essence, a Stone-Age culture for millennia, basically unchanging in almost all respects.

Then, "all of a sudden," we began to build cities, irrigate, farm, forge metals, develop written forms of recording things, create textiles, etc. Again, why then and not sometime in the countless millennia before then? Why just then?

4. Moreover, why does practically every culture in the world have legends of "sky gods," "sky guardians," or such, and always these religions and so-called myths say these others strongly influenced such civilizations' beginnings, or actively taught those early peoples the rudiments of civilization.

As just one of many examples, The Book of Enoch tells us Enoch was taken away and taught various things with regard to civilization, including how to work metals and how to write, and only then was he returned to the Earth. Furthermore, the texts imply he was gone for years, decades, if not centuries, before returning. (Relativistic travel speeds caused this, perhaps?)

5. Another strong piece of evidence is that from this same time forward, human history abounds with strange images, odd sculptures, bizarre pictographs, outlandish drawings, and weird paintings that strongly resemble alien spacecraft and aliens.

6. Legends and myths also abound, worldwide and not just regionally, of stories of strange creatures having a powerful influence on humanity. Whether we're talking of fairies, gnomes, leprechauns, trolls, ogres, giants, sky gods, sky guardians, Kachina beings, angels or aliens, these tales proliferate in every culture around the globe.

7. Ancient oddities throughout history concern the Moon and interactions with it. These are in the form of written and oral texts. *And as Anthony Roberts once said:*

"Legends are like time-capsules that preserve their contents through ages of ignorance."

What are we talking about here? Well, let's take a look at some of these, country by country. For example:

Tibet. In a remote region of Tibet, at some ancient ruins there, an explorer by the name of Duparc discovered in 1725 some huge monoliths, but also a large white stone. Surrounding this stone, were detailed, intricate drawings. Not knowing the language, Duparc had no idea what they meant or might have referred to. This in itself wouldn't be that big of a deal, except a later expedition, in 1952 was allowed to see sacred documents at a nearby Tibetan monastery.

The documents are purported to have described a white stone *"brought from the Moon."* This stone was, of course, considered sacred. Had Duparc come across an actual piece of the Moon, deliberately brought to Earth, according to those ancient texts? The coincidence is a big one if this is not the case. Perhaps it's too big to just be coincidence

China. Historian/recorder Chuang Tzu in or around 300 B.C.E, wrote of a journey he supposedly made, one some 32,500 miles out into space, in his work, Travel To The Infinite.

China again. An engineer in 2,309 B.C.E., one in the employ of Emperor Yao is said to have gone to the Moon. Moreover, he is said to have reached there by *"mounting the current of luminous air,"* which sounds VERY similar to a rocket's blast on takeoff. Also, once in space, "he did not perceive the rotary movement of the sun." This is highly significant. There is no rotary movement of the sun, because although people at the time believe it, the sun doesn't rotate around the Earth in actual fact, of course.

Tibet and Mongolia. Also out of Tibet, as well as Mongolia, ancient Buddhist texts speak of *"iron serpents which devour space with fire and smoke, reaching as far as the distant stars."*

Italy. Uncovered from beneath the Palatine Hill in Rome in 1961, a painting discovered there shows what looks very much like a rocket standing on a pad, ready to launch.

Greece. The writer/historian, Lucian, described the Moon as being much like the Earth in nature (round, spherical, etc.). He also wrote a story about it taking eight days to travel from the Earth to the Moon. Oddly, the first mission manned mission to the Moon, Apollo 11, took just about six days, so Lucian wasn't far off!

New Zealand. Machines capable of flying through the sky and taking trips to the Moon are profligate in ancient Maori tales.

Guatemala. There is a reference to a *"circular chariot of gold,"* measuring, roughly, 18,000 feet in circumference. It was said this "chariot" was *"able to reach the stars."*

Ancient Babylon. In the Epic of Etana, which is close to being 5,000 years old, there are oddly specific and accurate tales of how the Earth looks from on high, from different altitudes. Mind you, these descriptions couldn't be corroborated as correct until we, ourselves, attained (and then only in the last century) the ability to fly so high.

India. Here's a country that seems to have a wealth of information regarding such strange things as UFOs and aliens. In ancient texts, the Vedic Texts, are described craft said to have been able to orbit or "revolve" around the planet. The texts further claimed energy or fuel was extracted from the atmosphere in a simple and inexpensive way to power the vehicles. The only way the motors could fail was if they were deliberately turned off or damaged, otherwise, they could fly indefinitely.

Pretty detailed for a "mere myth," isn't it? If our historians had written something like this, we'd have thought they were telling the literal truth. Cultural bias does sometimes have a way of interfering with scientific progress, it would seem, by something as simple as what we choose to take seriously, and what we dismiss as being merely "fairy tales."

Furthermore, the text of the ***Mahabharata*** speaks of:

"Two-story, sky chariots with many windows, ejecting red flame, that race up into the sky until they look like comets [and travel] to the regions of both the sun and the stars."

Again, some explicit details here, as well, for something that is supposed to be just the stuff of legends and nothing more.

And there is more. The texts also talk of ancient scientists or alchemists who actually circled our planet *"below the Moon and above the clouds."* This is referenced to in the Surya Siddhanta. Moreover, huge satellite-like vessels made of "metal" and spinning on an axis are talked about in detail in the Vedic Texts. Flying saucers? They sure sound like it.

In addition, when we say detailed, we mean detailed! Information is given as to size, types of internal layout, power supplies, engines, crew quarters, etc. The texts specifically mention other vehicles used to travel back and forth from Earth to the "satellites." Again, the amount of detail for something supposedly just a legend is incredible.

Ancient Sumerian. Cuneiform writings talk about three items, a "golden sphere," a long, spear-like item with three sections, and a "alikmahrati." The translation of this last means *"that which makes the vessel move."* When combined, these items create an object that strongly resembles a three-stage rocket.

The long-term idea of aliens having been here. There is also credible evidence to support the idea the Moon (and aliens) have been here for a very long time. If one ignores the cultural references to the Moon having suddenly appeared in our skies, and if one is to believe any of the current multiple theories of how long the Moon has been here, then visitors from another star system may have arrived here ages ago, literally.

Besides the anecdotal evidence we've already provided as to why they might have come and wanted to stay early on in Earth's history, there are other factors:

1. Remember; some of the material on the Moon seems closely to resemble the structural makeup of the Earth's crust. This may be because such an alien race mined Earth's crust to create the outer layer of the Moon, to provide a "surface" to hide their true surface, the interior metal shell. After all, being so close to the Earth would make it a convenient place to perform such an operation. And what better concealment could they ask for?

2. There would seem to be some evidence that something has been happening on the Moon for a very long time. If there are ancient bases, antediluvian mining operations on the far side of the Moon, this would suggest the alien presence predates human civilization by a lot.

Are there such bases, abandoned ones, on the far side of the Moon? Well, we've mentioned this earlier in the book, named some of the people who believe it to be so, and the information they say proves it, as well as listing reference sites for images of these. It is up to you, the reader, to decide for yourself. However, we think it might very likely be probable. Either that, or some very renowned people, including astronauts and officials, must be lying through their teeth and also faked photographs into the bargain. We would hope sincerely this is not the case. Hoaxes and such are never a good idea. They cloud and act to obfuscate truths.

3. If mining operations on Earth date back as far as some people claim, including up to 250 million years ago in South Africa, the aliens have been around for a very long time.

4. We also have to consider all those so-called, "archaeological anomalies," that have been discovered over the last couple of hundred years. Everything from strange hand bells with bizarre gods engraved in the handle, a vase and ladle locked inside of coal, nails embedded in rock, hammers that are partially fossilized, then we have to consider that an alien influence has been on the Earth not just for thousands of years, or even tens of thousands, but perhaps for millions of years or more.

5. Then there is the matter of the so-called "missing link." Historically, archaeologists simply cannot account for the sudden appearance of modern man. Although we have found numerous offshoot species, or sub-species, if you will, we have not found a direct line, a direct series of links from the more primitive Homo Sapiens to the modern Cro-Magnon, which is us, of course. Even after over 200 years of searching, we have not found this missing link. Are we an altered species? As the many legends of the sky gods seem to say, are we the result of their direct interference? It just might be possible. Some say, this is even probable.

Chapter Conclusion. So it does seem no matter how one looks at it, the aliens have been here a long time. The only questions seems to be how long? Whether the duration is a matter of thousands, tens of thousands, or millions of years, is hard to say.

Again, there seems to be reasonable evidence to support both such hypotheses. In either case, it would seem to make little difference to us, as humans. Whichever scenario we choose, both seem to cover the entire span of human civilization, clear back to its very origins. And for us, this is enough. Regardless of which time span we choose, it means aliens have been influencing us for as long as humanity can remember, and perhaps longer.

But why are they here? Why do aliens move a satellite into orbit around the Earth, and wish to rule our skies? Why might we be so important? In the next chapter we will attempt to answer this.

CHAPTER 26
The Reason They're Here

Why are aliens here? Well in an earlier chapter, we discussed the idea it might be life, itself, attracting them. Despite the xenophobia we feel they most probably have, and which may well account for what we see as very secretive ways on their part, it may be they still wish to seek out new species, even so. This is a reasonable assumption given the evidence we've gathered so far.

However, because of their xenophobia, we must modify this to some degree. If after thousands of years of traveling in their hollow worlds, they have developed such xenophobia, then they would have an instinctive and perhaps deep-rooted fear of any other species whose civilization/technology is more advanced than their own. To approach such species would present an unreasonable, an intolerable risk for them, in their estimation, in all likelihood.

So if they did seek out other forms of life, intelligent life or otherwise, it would have to be those forms that are inferior to themselves, at least as far as their capabilities go. By this, we mean us. Certainly, if we now have capabilities of seeing planets in other star systems, they would have the same. So they could find us more easily than we could find them.

With their more advanced abilities, they would almost certainly know, even at a great distance, if certain worlds might bear life. We are rapidly approaching that capability, as well, right now. Very soon, it may be possible, with the aid of a new sort of space telescope, that uses an "occulter" (the proposed New Worlds Mission) to see the atmospheres of other planets around other stars.

Spectral analysis would then show us if there is oxygen, as well as other elements in those atmospheres. Free oxygen would almost certainly be a sign there is life. So if we are on the verge of doing it, surely a more advanced species, such as our aliens, could as well.

Moreover, since our solar system had at least one world (Earth) where life developed, and possibly two (Mars), then our solar system would have provided an attractive reason (in their estimation) to visit here. The fact the moon of Mars, Phobos, might also be hollow would seem further to corroborate this idea, make it a more distinct possibility. They may have stopped there first.

Added to this also remember, our solar system's Oort cloud, Kuiper belt, and Asteroid Belt, would be a rich source of supplies, minerals, etc., for them. They would have multiple reasons to visit here, even if their xenophobia did preclude them wanting to seek out new life to any real extent. So these form good reasons why they may have come to our solar system.

There is another reason. If one lives in a hollow world, or worlds, one must have stable populations. This mean certain endeavors that require much larger populations would be problematic, difficult to accomplish, unless they had access to a bigger labor pool when needed. Likewise, their physical makeup may naturally limit their ability to function on other worlds.

Earth, for example, might have a heavier gravity than their home world did. It certainly is far heavier here than on the Moon. As said earlier in this book, the Moon has only 1/6th the Earth's gravity.

Or, perhaps our atmosphere may be too rich in oxygen or not rich enough for them? It may be there are missing trace gases they need to survive? Might there may be microbial life here that is a danger to them and their health, strange germs, perhaps? Who knows?

For any of these motives, they might well have needed a native population to do their work for them, as the Sumerian Anunnaki supposedly did thousands of years ago, creating us for those "sky guardian" masters. Or perhaps, they just like to have others work for them because it's easier. They don't have to get their hands dirty that way, as it were, don't have to go down into shafts for mining, etc. Gold comes easier to those who want it, when others have to dig it up for them.

Yet another explanation might be simply they need something else from us. With all the incredible number of claimed alien abductions of humans, perhaps it is something genetic they require from us, new blood, so to speak? Or, it could be something else, something even more ominous. Again, it's hard to say without more information.

Perhaps, this is their way of colonizing other worlds, by creating intelligent species, or making the native intelligent species more like themselves. In other words, they might be colonizing and conquering by creating surrogates of themselves, meaning us. And if we aren't "there," yet, it may be that eventually the plan is we will be at some point in the future. Again, many people claim genetic manipulation has been going on with regard to humans for countless generations and aliens are behind it. Maybe, they don't invade so much as create invaders to occupy a world; again, meaning us.

Once more, the truth is we simply don't know. We can only make guesses, and attempt to surmise their motives. Just how successful we are at these remains to be seen. We know this, however, if they are here and we do think they are, then they must have some motivation or motivations for being here. This would naturally follow. Admittedly, just saying they have motivations, though, isn't a lot of information.

Still, there are certain things we can tell about them, just by their behavior. For instance, the idea of them having xenophobia is more a probability than a possibility in our estimation. And there is another thing. They seem to reside principally upon our Moon. That in itself speaks of something rather singular.

Why? Well, why not just occupy the Earth outright? Why not just take it over directly? They would seem to have the power, the capabilities. So if they haven't, there must be reasons for this, as well.

We've already mentioned some. They may not find our world exactly to their taste, as far as living upon its surface goes. That's why we may be here, a "created race," as a substitute for themselves, to do their bidding or to represent them, as sort of an offspring of them. But there also may be another big reason.

And ***For The World Is Hollow And Aliens Rule The Sky***, seems to be a particularly appropriate title for this book, based on that reason. The title pretty much states it all, because, you see, it sums up just what the aliens may be doing here. They seem to be able to come and go at their pleasure, and there seems to be nothing we can do to stop them. At least, this seems to have been the case so far.

Another reason might be they simply no longer fear us, know us too well, know our capabilities, and so recognize we are no match for them. They may now think of our solar system as their permanent home, too. They may even think of it as "theirs," and not "ours."

In such a case, with their far superior technology, they may have no fear of us anymore and see us as being far beneath them, perhaps not even intelligent, at least as far as they would see intelligence. Cats and dogs have some intelligence, for instance, but we don't see them as being on our level in that regard, or even perhaps "conscious." Who knows? Perhaps that's the way they view us. In other words, they may feel completely at home here now, and considers themselves to have as much right to be here, as we do, if not more. And with their superior technology, how could we argue the point?

They might even predate our own existence here, and so have a truly valid claim to such a thing. If we are in some way there "offspring" and they are the "parents," of our race and so were here first, then who the solar system truly belongs to could well be a moot point. In our youthful arrogance, our naïveté, we just think it belongs to us. We could well be wrong about that.

Yet another explanation might be they are a retrograde culture. We've mentioned this before, but only in passing. Still, who knows how long any intelligent species can survive before it turns inward on itself? Xenophobia may just be the first sign of a decline, or it may be the primary motivator for such a phenomenon.

In any event, it is certainly conceivable an entire species occupying the interior of a worldlet might eventually, over many millennia or even millions of years, become retrograde, stagnant, and even decadent. They could begin to lose their initiative and so might simply cease to have the abilities of protecting themselves as they once did.

They could become more vulnerable. This isn't necessarily a good thing for us in such a situation, this possible vulnerability of theirs. It might simply make them more defensive, more likely to attack, or retaliate even over some trivial matter. When a people, whether human or alien, are frightened, they would probably react much the same way. That is, unless they are just so different from us we cannot fathom how they would behave at all. This is a possibility, but we feel it is most likely not a probability.

Why do we feel this? Well, if they were so alien that we simply couldn't understand or comprehend them at all to any real degree whatsoever, if they don't have any of the same motivations as we do, then it is unlikely they would even take to space. If they lack the motivation of curiosity as we humans have, why bother to explore, for instance? They wouldn't travel out into the universe. They would feel quite happy where they were to begin with, that is, if they could even feel happiness as we think of it at all.

No, if they don't share any of the motivations we do, any of the feelings or emotions we have at all, it is unlikely they would be here in the first place. Therefore, we can safely assume we must have some things in common with them. If they are exploring the galaxy, they must be doing so for some reason. We've already pointed out the dangers inherent in such exploration, with regard to alien and more powerful races attacking them. Why leave home just to stir up a hornet's nest of hostile aliens who may be bent on your genocide? One would have to have good reason, and one of those reasons is a desire to survive by spreading out through the galaxy or beyond.

However, if they are a retrograde species or culture, and thus have developed vulnerabilities they wouldn't otherwise have, this doesn't mean they no longer still have some access to their sciences, even if they may have lost much of the knowledge of them. For all we know, the spacecraft at their disposal today may have been in existence for a very long time. Their ability even to repair them now may be minimal. We simply don't know.

Yet even so, they may still be powerful. We have to remember that a wounded animal can be far more dangerous than one that isn't. Are the aliens akin to a wounded animal in this way? Let's hope not!

Another alternative is perhaps they feel we have now developed to the point where their existence can be revealed, at least partially, or in stages to us. This could well be happening right now. Many people theorize this is exactly what is going on.

Maybe, they figure it's just time we knew they existed. However, this doesn't mean they still don't have reservations, perhaps, or even fears about us, so they may be proceeding with caution and taking their time. And time to them is a thing that doesn't need to be rushed. They think in the very long term, remember?

There are other implications, as well. As if their technological capabilities weren't far superior to our own, weren't enough, their control of the high ground only exacerbates that disparity of capabilities already existing between us. In the unlikely event of any war between us, not only could they rain down destruction anywhere on the face of the Earth without compunction, and very speedily, but we, on the other hand, would be seriously handicapped in any retaliation efforts in such an event.

Therefore, it would behoove us not to start such a thing. We couldn't win. We would most likely only come out the losers in such a situation, and our civilization shattered, maybe for good. Maybe our government knows this already.

We must emphasize this fact one more; the aliens most likely think in the long term. If a few humans survived a war with them and then must start over, that is of little consequence to the aliens. They can wait. Apparently, they have. So whatever relationship they have with us, or want to have with us now, if it doesn't work out, they can simply start over again. What are we saying here? Well, to be blunt, we humans exist on their terms and there is probably nothing we can do about it.

So why are the aliens here?

1. It may be natural, instinctive for intelligent species to spread throughout the universe, simply as a matter of survival instinct. As mentioned, the long-term chances of survival are greatly enhanced by doing this.

2. Population pressures may also add to this need to spread out through the galaxy. They just may need more resources and more habitats for them to occupy.

3. Fear of other powerful alien races attacking them and destroying the one planet they occupy and thus extinguishing them as a species might also be an incentive to travel to the stars, to spread out through the Milky Way, and create a diaspora. This would also help ensure their survival as a species, as well.

4. Planets are inherently dangerous. Their home world or any planet in general, may be considered by them as an unsafe place to exist. Again, they may follow the motto of "not putting "all their eggs in one basket."

After all, their home world, as with ours, is undoubtedly subject to earthquakes, tsunamis, storms, volcanoes, asteroid or comet impacts. It doesn't stop there, for there is the possibility of destructive solar flares from their sun, destruction by nearby cosmic ray bursts, exploding stars (novae, supernovae, and hypernovae) or even something so mundane as an asteroid impacting on a relatively nearby neutron star, which can cause the equivalent of a cosmic ray burst and a big one!

Such a devastating burst would hit without warning, without any way to prepare because they travel at the speed of light. So there is nothing one can do to protect against such a catastrophe, except one thing, and that is to live inside a protective shell, one that insulates against such a disastrous, sudden, and total irradiation. It is safer, therefore, to live inside a world than out on its surface.

So there are a host of intrinsic dangers when one is restricted to life on just one world, any number of means by which, over time, a species might be made extinct.

5. They may simply be curious. We, as a species, already are. Therefore, why shouldn't they be the same, maybe even more so?

6. Then there is the more hostile motivation. Besides just wanting to survive the attack of another powerful alien species, they may be actually hostile in their own right. They may want to spread through the galaxy to actively seek out other civilizations and destroy them, subjugate them, or put them to some use for their own enigmatic purposes.

This might just be the case with us. Many Ufologists claim that just this sort of thing might be happening to us, right now. If tens of thousands or more people are being abducted without any say in the matter by aliens, and many believe this to be true, as well, then something is definitely going on. Worse, it's going on without our permission. Our "inalienable" human rights are being ignored in the process by the aliens. And we don't even have any idea of why we're being abducted in such great numbers.

Chapter Conclusion. So, to sum up this chapter, there is any number of reasons, or combinations of them, for why the aliens might be here. It could be for survival purposes, curiosity, or an intention to dominate, or use us as a subservient labor pool, or even a combination of these things. We simply can't be sure. But that they are here seems to be a certainty.

CHAPTER 27

How Did The Moon Get Here?

To sum up what we've said here, let's briefly consider our main points, but first one that we haven't really discussed yet and that is just how did the Moon manage to get here, if it didn't form here on its own?

Well, obviously it needed some form of propulsion. Just what the propulsion system would be is a matter of conjecture. One would assume, based on our current technological abilities, that it would have to be "beyond our present capabilities" to move such a massive moon, although we do have the means to move smaller asteroids, if we so chose to do.

However, fusion power, which we are developing, might be one method of propulsion. Remember, the Moon has a lot of Helium 3, which is highly suitable as a fuel for fusion reactors, and we do have fusion reactors. They just don't yet put out enough energy to make them commercially feasible, compared to the energy put into them, as yet. But the aliens may have solved this problem long ago.

There is also antimatter. Yes, we can produce it ourselves but in very, very tiny amounts. However, aliens might have found a better method. They might well be able to produce it in much greater quantities.

Also, there is fission power, which we do have now and we do use. This is the messiest of the three methods, because of radioactive byproducts, but it does work and works well. Any of these methods may have been used.

Mind you, the Moon wouldn't move very fast, not at first. Its velocity would increase only very slowly, incrementally using such methods, but over time, a great deal of it, and the aliens seem to have plenty of that, the Moon could attain truly remarkable speeds if the acceleration were continuous.

Of course, there may be other methods we haven't thought of, other types of power we simply don't know exist yet. For instance, if "dark energy" could be harnessed somehow, that would certainly give them a means of propulsion and a limitless one at that. We just don't know.

Now people would ask, if this is so, then where are the engines, the "rockets that propelled the Moon?" Why don't we see them on the Moon?

Well, if the propulsion method is unknown to us, we don't really know what to look for along those lines, do we? If it is dark energy, for instance, how would that work? What type of engines, if any, would it require to function with such a power source? Or alternatively, perhaps they've somehow harnessed gravity to do their bidding, or have learned how to fold space. Again, for such an advanced race, we simply can't be sure of what they may be capable of doing. So we don't have any idea of what it is we would be looking for as a sign they used such methods of propulsion.

We must also take into account the Moon may have been "terraformed," modified after it was moved here. If this happened long ago, millions of years, that could account for the crust being similar in so many respects to Earth's crust. Again, maybe they mined the Earth to cover their "ship" and make it just resemble a natural heavenly body, "our" Moon? Maybe, they dismantled any obvious signs of the propulsion system over time? We just don't know.

Still, anyone who can move the equivalent of small planets around through interstellar space probably is capable of hiding the fact of how they do it. The Moon, after its long journey through the vast reaches of deep space may have had what amounts to a "retread" after its arrival, and so we no longer see the propulsion system. It may now be hidden. Again, we simply don't know.

Chapter Conclusion. How the Moon "got here" must remain a mystery for now. It is something that still waits for answers, for more exploration of the Moon to find these solutions. The question seems to be; do we ever intend to go back to find these answers, or have we truly been "warned off?"

CHAPTER 28
What To Make Of All This?

We have argued here about the premise the Moon may well be hollow, artificial to some degree, whether to a greater or lesser extent, we simply can't be sure. Whether it has just large caverns on it, or a true hollow interior is a matter for debate. However, we do think there is evidence to suggest the interior may well be hollow.

We've backed this argument with some interesting items of evidence that would seem to support our contention. And we think this evidence does support our theory and very well. To reiterate, briefly, the main items of evidence are:

1. The odd orbit of our Moon. The Moon's orbit is far too circular for comfort. Few mathematical constructions trying to model this explain how such an orbit came about by sheer chance, can account for it, at least, none adequately, other than it was just "extremely lucky." No standard explanation really can explain such a circular orbit.

The only explanation that really works well is the Moon was placed deliberately in such a circular orbit. Yet, this explanation is the one most scientists refuse to consider.

2. The origin of the Moon seems to be an enigma. Although the closest heavenly body to us, and long observed, and even physically explored on a number of occasions, by landing on the surface as well as having satellites orbit it, we still aren't sure how it was formed. We really don't know "how it got to be where it is." In other words, no one theory of its origin seems effectively to explain how it came to be, unless one resorts to our Hollow Moon and Alien Theory.

3. The density of the Moon presents major problems, as well. Based on current theories, the Moon should be hollow, at least to some extent. Otherwise, we simply can't account for its low density. The Hollow Moon Theory does.

4. The crust of the far side of the Moon, the side we can't see directly from Earth, is considerably thicker than the side facing us. This is very odd. What's more, the near side is the one that has the "seas," the "*maria*," where the far side doesn't. The far side has more craters than the nearer side. Our current origin theories for the Moon cannot account for these truly major oddities. The Hollow Moon Theory does.

5. Although the crust of the Moon, at least the outer crust, seems to have a composition very similar to that of Earth, there are some notable differences with regard to certain minerals/elements and the amounts of them. There simply are too many of them to be accounted for easily with the standard theories. However, if the Moon is an artificial construct, as in the Hollow Moon Theory, this would account for those discrepancies.

6. The Moon rings like a bell when anything strikes it, or lands on its surface. What's more, scientists have determined this just shouldn't be, given the current theories of the makeup of the Moon's core. In other words, again, our theories about the Moon seemed to be incorrect. However, maybe the Moon really is like a bell? It certainly rings like one. So perhaps the Hollow Moon Theory is correct.

7. The sighting of Transient Lunar Phenomena over the many centuries is also a major oddity. Most of these simply cannot be accounted for, unless a plethora of new theories are postulated for the different types of them. Remember, it would take more than one such theory to account for all the varieties of such anomalies. However, the Hollow Moon Theory would account for all of them. "Whoever" is inside is causing them.

8. The moon of Mars, Phobos, might well be hollow, as well, and if so could be yet another example of the Hollow Moon Theory. There may be more than one hollow moon in our solar system, and so this gives added support to the idea of the Hollow Moon Theory.

9. Testimony by astronauts, NASA employees, subcontractors to NASA, all seem to indicate there is some sort of alien influence/menace, with regard to near Earth space, around the Moon and even within the confines of our own atmosphere. This would lend support to the idea aliens may well be on or more likely, "in" the Moon. It would make the perfect base for such activity, give them the high ground. This, too, would lend more credence to the idea of the Hollow Moon Theory.

10. An incredible number of UFOs sightings by civilians and military, photographs, as well as testimony of various officials, along with numerous accounts of alien abductions, and animal mutilations, all seem to suggest we are being "visited." Again, more evidence to support the idea aliens might be nearby, and thus in a Hollow Moon.

11. Historical references to the Moon having suddenly appeared in our sky near the dawn of recorded history, or even prior to it, and by many cultures around the world, would also lend credence to the idea of the Moon being a spaceship, and so acts to support the idea of the Hollow Moon Theory.

Given all this, we feel there is an incredible amount of information, evidence, and facts to back the idea the Moon may be hollow, or at least have large hollow cavities within it. That the Moon may be, at least in part, an artificial construct, is an idea that simply shouldn't be dismissed out of hand, not by any means, not given all this data and evidence.

And if the Moon is hollow, as may be Phobos, as well, and this is the result of being artificially made so, which seems to be far more likely than it somehow occurring naturally, then we must assume some intelligent hand guided the processes. Since we cannot possibly be the intelligent hand that did this, we must assume it is an alien one.

Moreover, we've clearly demonstrated that with all the Earth-like planets in our galaxy alone, numbering in the millions if not billions, that life, and alien life, according to most scientists, is now considered a major probability, rather than just a mere possibility. We've also demonstrated here that if such species do exist, many of them must have come into being millions, if not a few billion years before we did.

Furthermore, we've demonstrated if such species do come into being, and this would seem to be the situation, then eventually they would want to attain the ability to travel to the stars. We've shown here one of the easiest ways to do this is via hollowing out asteroids, and/or worldlets.

We've further shown the ability to move these asteroids; at least some of them, out of our solar system into interstellar space is not even beyond our own current capabilities, let alone that of an alien species, whose technological prowess may be way beyond our own.

Therefore, we think, based on all this evidence, the Moon may, indeed, be hollow! There may indeed be aliens inhabiting it even now, or have inhabited it in the past. We certainly think this idea merits more investigation.

After all, if scientists cannot come up with a satisfactory theory to account for the origin of our Moon, or its current physical makeup with any accuracy, and so keep coming up with new ones, even as recently as just a couple of years ago, then we must consider other options.

As Sir Conan Doyle's fictional character, Sherlock Holmes, said, *"When one has excluded all the possible explanations, then one must look to the impossible."* Since we can't seem to find any other answers that fit the conditions of our Moon, we have chosen to do just this, and we don't think the idea of a Hollow Moon Theory is really so very impossible. And neither do many of the scientists we've mentioned by name here.

As we've shown in this book, For The Moon Is Hollow And Aliens Rule The Sky, the idea of the Moon being hollow isn't impossible at all. In fact, it could well be quite probable. And if it is, then we have other major concerns to consider regarding the future well-being of the human species here on planet Earth. To overlook the ramifications of these considerations, the possible deadly consequences such a refusal to do so might cause, would be very foolish indeed.

If humans are to survive in the long term, then we, just as many other alien species probably already have done, must consider all the ramifications of everything around us. We need to consider what adds to our survival capabilities and also what detracts from them. Having a world so close to us, perhaps a hollow one, as with our Moon, and perhaps one filled with an alien species that may or may not be hostile to us, is certainly something worth considering under such circumstances.

In conclusion, just let us say we think there is a real possibility, a very real possibility that the Moon is either hollow as some scientists have suggested, or at least contains large caverns, most likely artificially created or enhanced in size. We further think, given the massive amount of evidence, aliens now inhabit, or have inhabited these inner regions of the Moon.

We also feel they are "interfering" with us in a big way. Here, we've attempted to explain where "they" came from, how exactly they may have arrived here, where they may be living, as well as what motivates them and their basic attitudes toward us. We've tried to show how those very attitudes have been shaped by their own evolution, and long travels through interstellar space.

Our perceptions of reality color how we think of the possibility of an alien intelligent life may have formed. For countless millennia, we have felt we were the only such species, that we were unique. We have, perhaps quite erroneously, thought we were the "top of the food chain."

Well, maybe we are not. Just maybe, it's time to rethink that whole concept. If we've even done that much here, to make the reader reconsider their attitudes as to what is possible and even probable when it comes to extraterrestrial life, and how such a species might view other aliens (meaning us), then we feel we have succeeded in this endeavor.

One thing more; if alien species feel it necessary to enter a "diaspora" phase of existence, to leave their home worlds behind and start an endless journey though the stars as a long-term survival strategy, then someday very soon, we might just do the same. Therefore, it would seem incumbent upon us to develop the appropriate attitudes, just as they have had to do in order to successfully accomplish such an incredible endeavor.

This doesn't mean we should "run in panic" at the sight of an alien being. It does mean, however, we should remember that even among humans, not all are our "brothers and sisters," and that some humans mean harm to others. Even as aliens have probably acquired this precaution when dealing with other species, so should we. We should not go blindly "into that good night."

So if ever we meet another intelligent species, instead of fleeing in blind fear, or welcoming them unquestioningly with open arms, perhaps we should do the adult thing. Maybe, we should stop, pause long enough to think things through, to consider the possible ramifications of it all, and then proceed with caution.

Don't we do the same thing when we meet a stranger in a dark alley at night? Why then, shouldn't we do it with strangers who come from out of the endless dark night, the eternal darkness of interstellar space?

Of course, we may just have to learn to "all get along." This may be especially so if aliens inhabit our Moon, dominate our night skies, and look down upon us with unknown intentions. Under such circumstances, in the final analysis, we may simply have no choice, no alternative left to us. We may have to comply, because as one line from **Star Trek** put it, it might just be that "resistance is futile."

We might, finally, realize we are not the masters of all we survey. We may discover we are not at the top of the food chain after all. This last lesson may be the hardest of all the lessons for us to learn, and even harder yet for us to live with. For rather than being the ultimate predators in our solar system, perhaps, just perhaps, we are the ultimate prey?

ABOUT THE AUTHOR

Rob Shelsky is an avid and eclectic writer, and averages about 4,000 words a day. Rob, with a degree in science, has written a large number of factual articles for the former AlienSkin Magazine, as well as for other magazines, such as Doorways, Midnight Street (U.K.), Internet Review of Science Fiction (IROSF), and many others. While at AlienSkin Magazine, a resident columnist there for about seven years, Rob did a number of investigative articles, including some concerning the paranormal, as well as columns about UFOs, including interviews of those who have had encounters with them.

He has often and over a long period, explored the Alien and UFO question and has made investigative trips to research such UFO hotspot areas as Pine Bush, New York, Gulf Breeze, Florida, and other such regions, including Brown Mountain, North Carolina, known, for the infamous "Brown Mountain Lights, as well as investigating numerous places known for paranormal activity.

With over 20 years of such research and investigative efforts behind him, Author Rob Shelsky is well qualified in the subject of UFOs, as well as that of the paranormal. Where Rob Shelsky tends to be the skeptic, and insists upon being able to "kick the tires" of a UFO, to ascertain their reality, he is, as well, a theorist, constantly coming up with possible explanations for various such phenomena. Rob asks the hard questions others seem to avoid. Often, he comes up with convincing answers.

For links to other books written, please go to

http://home.earthlink.net/~robngeorge/

Or: http://robshelsky.blogspot.com/

Or:
http://www.amazon.com/gp/search/ref=sr_tc_2_0?rh=i%3Astripbooks%2Ck%3ARob+Shelsky&keywords=Rob+Shelsky&ie=UTF8&qid=1298820526&sr=1-2-ent&field-contributor_id=B002BO9RIE

REFERENCES

http://www.ancient-code.com/alien-Moon-base-in-official-nasa-images/#sthash.WT1eIeQh.dpuf
http://beforeitsnews.com/beyond-science/2013/01/alien-base-on-the-Moon-in-detail-clear-ufo-photos-released-by-nasa-taken-by-astronauts-pilot-films-ufo-from-air-2440716.html
http://www.solarviews.com/cap/Moon/Moondust.htm
http://www.veteranstoday.com/2013/01/09/congressionial-disclosure-studies-alien-Moon-bases/
http://answers.yahoo.com/question/index?qid=20081202140152AA88qxs
http://disinfo.com/2010/09/who-parked-the-Moon/
http://www.incredipedia.info/2012/02/hollow-Moon-alien-base.html
http://www.examiner.com/article/thirteen-ufos-launch-from-Moon-alleges-astronomer
http://www.alien-ufos.com/armageddon-end-times/29705-hollow-Moon.html
http://alienufoparanormal.aliencasebook.com/2008/08/09/hollow-Moon-theory-rings-a-bell--micah-a-hanks.aspx
http://cryptid.hubpages.com/hub/Is-the-Moon-Hollow-Evidence-Supporting-Hollow-Moon-Theory
http://ufodigest.com/article/scientist-claims-mars-Moon-phobos-hollow
http://www.astroscience.org/abdul-ahad/Earth-ring.htm
http://dad2059.wordpress.com/2012/09/17/score-one-for-hollow-Moon-theory/

http://www.themortonreport.com/discoveries/paranormal/aliens-on-the-Moon/
http://en.wikipedia.org/wiki/Hollow_Moon
http://beforeitsnews.com/alternative/2010/12/nasa-photos-confirm-moon-is-artificial-317206.html
http://www.abovetopsecret.com/forum/thread808412/pg1
http://en.wikipedia.org/wiki/Internal_structure_of_the_Moon
http://evolutionwiki.org/wiki/Short-lived_isotopes_Th-230_and_U-236_exist_on_the_moon
http://www.space.com/13247-moon-map-lunar-titanium.html
http://news.discovery.com/space/history-of-space/moon-titanium-111012.htm
http://www.bibliotecapleyades.net/marte/marte_phobos01.htm
http://www.universetoday.com/58923/could-phobos-be-hollow/
http://www.nasa.gov/mission_pages/msl/news/msl20130312.html
http://www.examiner.com/article/is-this-new-evidence-for-ancient-life-on-mars
http://www.npr.org/blogs/thetwo-way/2014/03/26/294872989/for-the-first-time-astronomers-find-asteroids-can-have-rings
http://www.space.com/51-asteroids-formation-discovery-and-exploration.html
http://www.windows2universe.org/the_universe/uts/moon1.html
http://www.windows2universe.org/the_universe/uts/moon1.html
http://csep10.phys.utk.edu/astr161/lect/moon/moon_formation.html
http://www.livescience.com/33883-gallery-weird-moon.html
http://www.bibliotecapleyades.net/luna/esp_luna_26.htm

http://www.thelivingmoon.com/43ancients/02files/Moon_Others_01.html
http://www.abovetopsecret.com/forum/thread924918/pg1
http://paranormal.about.com/od/lunaranomalies/ig/Strange-Things-on-the-Moon/
http://www.ufosightingsdaily.com/
http://www.huffingtonpost.com/tag/ufo-sightings
http://www.latest-ufo-sightings.net/
http://www.syti.net/UFOSightings.html
http://www.ufostalker.com/
http://nyufo.bravesites.com/
http://www.mirror.co.uk/news/weird-news/bizarre-alien-base-spotted-google-304262
http://www.bibliotecapleyades.net/vida_alien/esp_vida_alien_37.htm
http://www.huffingtonpost.com/2014/01/27/is-there-an-alien-base-on-the-moon_n_4632986.html
http://www.rense.com/general70/rep.htm
http://www.theepochtimes.com/n3/462497-huge-alien-object-spotted-on-moon-via-nasa-imaging-photos/
http://ufodigest.com/news/0708/ancient-moon2.html
http://www.google.com/url?sa=t&rct=j&q=&esrc=s&source=web&cd=1&ved=0CCkQFjAA&url=http%3A%2F%2Fexopolitics.org%2Ffirst-man-on-moon-dies-along-with-secrets-of-what-he-saw%2F&ei=gtc5U_uiEubhsASJkYKADQ&usg=AFQjCNGt3fecCFoliF5VGJQN02dKDzVE2w&sig
http://www.ufocasebook.com/moon.html2=frKPFbDrZ0U0qvjUfHKnug&bvm=bv.63808443,d.cWc

Made in the USA
San Bernardino, CA
04 August 2014